FOREVER FREE

Elsa's Pride

JOY ADAMSON

Forever Free

Elsa's Pride

Collins
FONTANA BOOKS

First published 1962
First issued in Fontana Books 1966
Eleventh Impression December 1971

© Joy Adamson, 1962

Printed in Great Britain
Collins Clear-Type Press
London and Glasgow

*To all who help in
the conservation of wild life*

INTRODUCTION

Born Free told the story of Elsa; *Living Free* told the story of Elsa and her cubs during their first year; *Forever Free* tells of the last months of Elsa's life, of her death, so movingly described by George Adamson, and of what happened to the cubs after they had lost their mother, involving both them and the Adamsons in many hazardous adventures which make this last volume most exciting reading.

I feel particularly close to the Elsa story, because ever since I met Joy Adamson in the spring of 1959, when she had come to London to plan the publication of *Born Free*, she has sent me frequent reports. First they were about all that happened at Elsa's camp, then about the birth and growth of the cubs; after Elsa's death, they described the many problems which arose.

I had also the opportunity of making two unforgettable visits to the Adamsons in their camp where, for a short time, I shared the life they led by the river Ura. The late afternoon was the most interesting part of the day, for then we walked out to look for Elsa and the cubs. After we had found them we all returned together to camp and the lions spent the evening and the night there. At dawn I used to wake and see them departing to take cover during the hot hours.

The first two books about Elsa have been translated into fifteen languages, for her story seems to have caught the imagination of people of all ages and interests.

The following letter gives a picture of the affection in which she was held:

> 912 *North Madison Avenue,*
> *Jonesboro, Arkansas,*
> *January the 30th, 1961*

My dear Mr. Prime Minister:
The story of Elsa, the lioness of fame in *Born Free* by

Mrs. George Adamson, has captivated the hearts and minds of many people in this area. It is currently appearing in serial form in the Memphis *Commercial Appeal*. An additional story was carried yesterday in the Tennessee paper of Elsa's death last Tuesday, January 24th, 1961, at her Kenya home.

Although we are thousands and thousands of miles from the scene of this tragedy, there are several of us in Arkansas who would like to have glossy photographs of Elsa during her lifetime and would, therefore, thank you to ascertain and advise us the mailing address of her mistress. No other animal's death in memory has caused such an emotional upset of the population as has that of that lovable lioness.

We thank you in advance for your courtesy in the matter.

Very truly yours,
[Signed] W. R. Cunningham

The Honourable Harold Macmillan,
Prime Minister of Great Britain,
No. 10 Downing Street,
London, England.

On Christmas Day 1960, just before *Forever Free* opens, the Adamsons received a request to remove Elsa and her cubs from the reserve in which they were living. This set them grave problems, but these were nothing compared to those which they had to face when after Elsa's death the cubs disappeared.

The account of their finding the cubs and of how, eventually, they managed to trap them for their long journey to the Serengeti, where they had been offered a new home, is a dramatic one. I can remember the anxious days I spent during a business visit to New York in April 1961, waiting for a cable. It arrived the day before my return and read: 'Cubs successfully trapped.' What a relief that was, for by then they were under a suspended death sentence.

The Serengeti is ideal lion territory and once the cubs had

made the seven-hundred-mile drive to their new home, the Adamsons had every right to expect that all would be well. But things did not turn out as they anticipated and the story is full of ups and downs.

The trouble arose as the result of an incident which took place during the weeks after Elsa's death, when the cubs had disappeared from the reserve and the Adamsons had lost touch with them. Almost starving, for they had not yet learned to hunt, they raided some huts for food. The Africans went after them with bows and arrows; Jespah got hit and an arrow-head lodged in his rump. Fortunately it had been shot by a toto (a small African boy) too young to be allowed to use poisoned arrows. It proved impossible to remove the arrow-head before the cubs' release in the Serengeti; the Adamsons hoped it would work its way out, but when they saw the cubs again in July 1961 it was still embedded and Jespah didn't seem too well so they felt it was essential to try to have it re-moved. How they were hindered by red tape in getting this done is the sad part of this story.

In this book you will read of the hazards that they and the cubs met with and how on a number of occasions the Adam-sons' lives, as well as those of the lions, were in serious danger. In the winter of 1961-62 terrible floods dispersed all the animals; during these five months the Adamsons had many adventures, took great risks and faced grave dangers in their determined. but fruitless, effort to locate the cubs.

During all the months which the Adamsons have spent in the Serengeti they have seen a vast variety of wild life, especially at the time of the great trek when hundreds of thousands of animals cross the plain. This had given them the opportunity to take many beautiful and unusual photographs. These, some in black and white and others in colour, closely illustrate the text of the book. They are even better than those in the previous volumes; two are outstanding: one is of Jespah lying on the top of Joy's Land-Rover, the other shows him looking at his own image in the windscreen. The Land-Rover had been one of Elsa's favourite places and it had surprised the Adamsons that Jespah, who was so close to his mother, had never tried to get on to the car. On the first day of the last week in which they saw the cubs he did so. This was after he had been shot at, had endured a seven-hundred-mile journey and had for weeks lived wild with his brother and sister. That, now, he should suddenly imitate his mother's behaviour shows that her instinct was deep in him.

These photographs bring back vivid memories to me for during the last night I spent in Elsa's camp she broke through a thorn fence and lay for part of the night on top of the Land-Rover inside which I was sleeping.

Some two months after these photographs were taken I spent a week with Joy Adamson in the Serengeti, during which we tried to locate the cubs and see whether Jespah still carried the arrowhead. We were unsuccessful, but I left knowing that the cubs had a perfect home and that it was full of game. Now, as I write, the Adamsons are back in the Serengeti, searching again under better weather conditions and one can only hope that this time they will be successful. I am sure that all readers of this book will long to hear that the cubs have been seen, that the arrowhead has worked out and that all three are living, *forever free*, the kind of life for which the Adamsons have fought for so long and with such courageous determination to secure for them.

W. A. R. Collins
AUGUST, 1962

CONTENTS

ILLUSTRATIONS

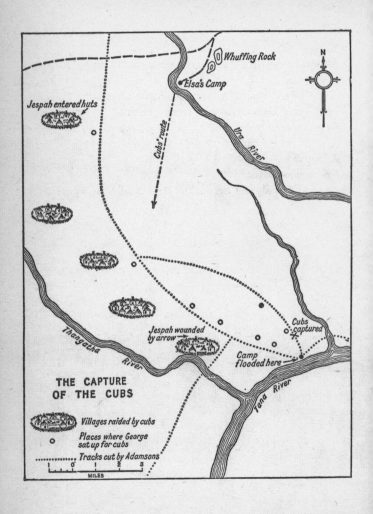

Whuffing Rock

Elsa's Camp

Ura River

Jespah entered huts

Cubs' route

Jespah wounded
by arrow

Cubs
captured

Camp
flooded here

Thangatha River

Tana River

THE CAPTURE
OF THE CUBS

Villages raided by cubs

Places where George
sat up for cubs

Tracks cut by Adamsons

0   1   2   3
MILES

N

Chapter One

THE DEPORTATION ORDER

IT WAS ON Christmas Eve 1960 that we received a letter from the African District Council ordering us to remove Elsa and her cubs from the reserve. The reason given by the council was that since Elsa was used to our company she might become a danger to other people.

We were amazed; the local authorities themselves had helped us to choose the area for her release, and up to now had regarded her as a great asset to the reserve. It had been her home for two and a half years, and during that time she had never hurt anyone. We were as anxious as they were to avoid the possibility of an accident, and had even offered to pay a good rent for Elsa's territory, so that visitors could be kept out of it without financial loss to the game reserve.

Now, with the arrival of the deportation order, all we could do was to try to make this removal as little harmful to the lions as possible and find a satisfactory new home for them.

We wrote to friends in Tanganyika, Uganda, the Rhodesias and South Africa, inquiring what the chances were of finding a good territory for the family in their countries, but, before finally deciding to remove Elsa and her family from Kenya, George wished to carry out a reconnaissance along the eastern shores of Lake Rudolf in the north of Kenya.

I was distressed by this plan. The country there is very grim, and I feared that game around the lake might be so scarce that Elsa and the cubs would become dependent upon us for their food supply. Besides this, the area is so remote that in case of an emergency we should be very lucky if we were able to get any help. On the other hand, this very remoteness was an asset, for the fact that this country is inhospitable and almost cut off from the rest of Africa would at least ensure that the lions would be unlikely to become a pawn in political intrigues.

So, while we waited for replies to our letters, we made provisional plans for their removal to Lake Rudolf. We estimated that the journey would take two or three days and nights : we knew that the tracks would be very rough and that we should need to tow the cars through sandy river-beds, stretches of desert and over rocky escarpments.

When we had first moved Elsa to her release point, we had used a tranquilliser which proved too strong for her. Now she and her cubs had to make a long journey, we might again need tranquillisers. I therefore wrote to vets in Kenya, England, and the United States to get advice as to which was considered the safest for lions. We knew that we would have to give the drugs by mouth, at least to the cubs, who were too wild to allow us to use a hypodermic syringe. With this in mind, we decided that we must at once accustom them to feeding in a confined space. This would make it possible for us, later on, to control the amount of food and with it the dose which each cub got.

To make the experiment we would first build a ramp and then place a five-ton lorry against it so that its floor was level with the top of the ramp; in the lorry we would place the lions' dinner. Once the cubs had got used to their new feeding place we could build a strong wire enclosure over the lorry and make a trap door to it, which we would close when the cubs were feeding, thus converting the lorry into a travelling crate.

We dug the ramp at the salt-lick near the studio. My heart was heavy as I watched the cubs; they were excited by the unusual activities taking place on their playground, sniffed the freshly dug soil curiously, found it great fun to roll on the earth, and seemed to think that all this work was being done to amuse them.

On 28th December George left camp and after a few days at Isiolo started off on the recce to Lake Rudolf. That afternoon I met the family near the river, and after the usual friendly greetings from Elsa and Jespah, we went together to the water's edge. The cubs plunged in at once, ducking and chasing each other; Elsa and I watched them from the bank.

While they were in the river she guarded them in a dignified manner, but when they emerged dripping wet joined in their games and helped them to look for a new playground. A nearby tree provided what was needed, the cubs struggled up its trunk but were soon overtaken by their mother, who in a few swift movements leapt high above them. I gasped as she went higher and higher, the slender upper branches bending alarmingly beneath her weight finally she reached the crown of the tree. What, I wondered, was she doing? Teaching her children the proper way to climb trees, or just showing off? When she found that the boughs were no longer strong enough to support her, she turned with great difficulty and, cautiously testing each branch, began her descent. She managed to make her way down but her landing was by no means dignified, then, as though to suggest that the tumble was a joke, she at once began to jump around the cubs. They chased her, and all the way home played games of hide-and-seek or ambushes, in which I was often the victim.

Next day, at tea-time, Elsa showed me very clearly what a wonderful mother and companion she was to her cubs. The family appeared on the far bank of the river opposite the studio. I had seen a six-foot crocodile slither into the river at their approach and was therefore not surprised when the cubs paced nervously up and down the rocky platform by the river's edge, obviously frightened to jump into the deep pool beneath.

Elsa licked each in turn, then they all plunged in together and swam safely across in close formation. When the cubs relaxed and began to chase each other so as to get dry, Elsa joined in. She took Jespah's tail in her mouth and walked round in circles with him, obviously enjoying the clowning as much as he did.

Eventually Jespah sat down close to me, turning his back to me. This he did when he wanted to be petted; he seemed to realise that I was always a little afraid of being accidentally scratched by him because, unlike his mother, he had not learnt to retract his claws when playing with human beings.

When I went for an afternoon stroll, the lions joined me; I

welcomed this new habit of a family walk; it gave me a
chance to observe the cubs' reactions to everything we met on
our way and also allowed me to spend more time with Elsa,
of whose company I had been to a considerable extent deprived
since the birth of the cubs. When we reached the Big Rock,
Gopa and Little Elsa stayed behind; I tried to induce them to
follow us but they would not. Elsa walked along as if she
knew no harm would come to them. She had lately kept her
children on a longer leash and did not seem to worry when
they showed independence. Jespah, however, was plainly very
anxious; he ran backwards and forwards between us and only
eventually and with reluctance decided to follow his mother
and me.

We walked for about two miles; when it grew cooler, Elsa
and Jespah began to play; it was very funny to see each trying
to outwit the other as they gambolled about like kittens.

On our way back I saw Gopa and Little Elsa on a rocky out-
crop of the main ridge, silhouetted against a magnificent sunset. They watched me aloofly as I passed below them. Elsa
and Jespah climbed to the top of the Big Rock and called
softly. Lazily the two cubs stretched and yawned and then
joined their mother. All through the evening I waited with a
carcase, but there was no sign of Elsa or the cubs. Late at
night I heard the whuffings of the cubs' father which explained
their absence. Next morning, to make sure that all was well,
I went with Nuru to the rock; at the base we found the spoor
of a large lion.

For two days Elsa and the cubs kept away from the camp,
and during this time I repeatedly heard their father roaring.
When Elsa returned it was late in the evening. Only her sons
were with her, but she did not seem perturbed at Little Elsa's
absence, and after a large meal they all went back to the rock.

Early next morning I followed up their spoor until I saw
Gopa and Little Elsa on the rock; then, assuming that their
father might be nearby, I went home.

Later in the afternoon the whole family appeared along the
road. Gopa and Little Elsa were panting; they had been

chasing a jackal which I had heard calling some way off. While Elsa greeted me, I signalled to Nuru to return to camp and prepare a carcase, but Jespah decided that Nuru was to play hide-and-seek with him and, until his mother intervened, Nuru had to use all his wits to dodge the cub. Elsa then took her offspring in hand, played with them and kept them busy until Nuru's task was accomplished; she so often acted in this way that it was impossible not to conclude that she did so deliberately. When we arrived in camp, the cubs pounced on their dinner, but their mother seemed to be very nervous and after several short reconnaissances disappeared into the bush, leaving them behind.

On the first of January I felt very apprehensive. What would the New Year bring? As if to cheer me up, Jespah came close and, taking up his 'safety position' (i.e. the one that ensured my safety from his claws), invited me to play with him. I stroked him affectionately, but suddenly he rolled over and instinctively I jerked back. He looked bewildered, then again rolled into his safety position and tilted his head. Plainly he could not understand my fear of his unretracted claws; repeatedly he invited me to play with him, and I wished I could explain to him that when his mother was a tiny cub I had been able to teach her to control her claws, and that was why I could play with her fearlessly, but not with him.

The following day the same thing happened : Jespah wanted a game and I wanted to play with him, but when I came within reach of his claws I was obliged to break off. Elsa watched the scene from the top of the Land-Rover. She seemed to be aware of Jespah's disappointment at my cautious behaviour, for she came down and licked and hugged her son until he was happy again. Meanwhile Little Elsa sneaked around nervously, hiding in the grass and obviously too frightened by my presence to come out into the open. Elsa went over to her and rolled about with her until she too was quite at her ease. When Jespah and Gopa joined in the fun Elsa retired to her sanctuary on top of the Land-Rover; I went up to her, intending to stroke her to make up for the apparent unfriendliness I had shown towards her son; but when I approached she spanked me, and during the whole of that evening she remained aloof.

On the 2nd of January, Ken Smith and Peter Saw, both game wardens from adjoining districts, arrived in a lorry. They had come with the consent of the Game Department to offer their help in moving Elsa and the cubs. Ken took some measurements for fitting the ramp to a four-wheel-drive Bedford lorry belonging to the Government, which he proposed to lend us for the move. He also offered to order a lion-proof wire enclosure to fit it, and to send us our old Thames lorry until the adjustments to the Bedford were completed. This would make it possible for us to accustom the cubs to feeding in a lorry with the minimum loss of time.

Ken had been on the lion hunt which brought Elsa into our life and had visited her twice since then, but he had never seen the cubs, so, after we had dealt with the measurements, we all went off to look for the family. We found them in the studio lugga ('lugga' is Somali for dry river bed), but at the sight of two strangers the cubs bolted. Elsa greeted Ken as an old friend, but paid no attention to Peter. She put up with being photographed, but when our guests came close to her, Jespah peeped anxiously through the foliage, obviously prepared to defend his mother if the need arose. Eventually he came into the open, though he kept at a safe distance from Ken and Peter.

As we did not want to upset the cubs, we returned to camp and sent the lorry a few hundred yards down the track. A little later Elsa arrived alone. She watched us for some time and then, still ignoring Peter, she gripped Ken firmly around the knee with her paw; we guessed she wanted to show him that she thought it was time for him to go. Ken took the hint and they left, and immediately the cubs came bouncing along and began to play. This showed us that they were becoming increasingly shy of strangers. Jespah had overcome his suspicion of George and myself, but he didn't trust anyone else.

He showed his confidence in me on the following day, when he allowed me to remove a tick from his eyelid and rid him also of a couple of maggots. These pests are fairly common in a low-lying, semi-desert country. The mango fly deposits her eggs by preference in wet or at least damp places. Any animal walking over or rolling on the spot may pick up the eggs, which develop into tiny maggots. After the skin has been perforated by a maggot, a swelling the size of a cherry develops. When the maggot has grown to about half an inch, it drops out through the hole made when the skin was originally perforated; afterwards it develops into a pupa and finally into the mango fly. The process of developing under the skin takes about ten days and during the later stages is very irritating and painful to its host. The animal tries to rid itself of the parasite by licking and scratching the wound, thus usually infecting it. In Elsa's case I sometimes found that her rough tongue removed the maggot's protruding head, with the result that the body, which remained under the skin, decomposed and caused sepsis. I used to try to prevent this by pressing the maggot out as soon as its head appeared. It was a rather disagreeable process, but it spared her real pain and the risk of infection later on. These maggots, which are found in great numbers in most game animals, though themselves harmless, weaken the condition of their host and render it susceptible to other illnesses.

Jespah kept absolutely still while I attended to his maggots, then he licked his wounds and placed himself in his safety position, inviting me to pat him. For the first time, he even allowed me to touch his silky nostrils; perhaps he wanted to show me that he was grateful for my help.

That evening he came alone into the tent, squatted in his safety position, and kept quite still until I stroked him. His demands for affection posed a serious problem: I hated to disappoint him but, on the other hand, apart from my fear of his claws, we wanted the cubs to develop into wild lions, and Jespah's friendliness was already jeopardising his future. Gopa and Little Elsa were different; their reactions were always those of wild animals.

Jespah was the leader of the cubs. One afternoon I found him in great distress; he was alone on the far bank of the river, which the rest of the family had just crossed; he was pacing up and down looking anxiously at the water, obviously scared by the presence of a crocodile. I tried to help him by throwing sticks and stones into the deep pool across which he had to swim, but he only pulled faces at the invisible reptile. After a time, however, he made up his mind, plunged in and swam as fast as he could, deliberately churning up the water. Elsa, standing quite still a few yards off, had watched my attempts to frighten the crocodile away. When Jespah had landed safely, she came over and licked me affectionately; he too was particularly friendly all that afternoon.

In the evening, as we were walking up the narrow path to the tents, Gopa ambushed me, growling savagely; I was quite frightened, and could not think what had caused him to be so cross, until I saw that he had taken his dinner to this spot, and realised that when I passed within a few feet of the 'kill' he had felt obliged to defend it.

The next day the Thames lorry arrived. We gave it a thorough wash and then parked it at the ramp, but it smelt of petrol, oil and Africans, and nothing would persuade the cubs to go near it. Even Elsa would not follow me into it, although I tried every trick I could think of to persuade her, in the belief that her example would encourage the cubs. There was nothing to be done except to wait until the lions had overcome their suspicion of the lorry, and remind myself that since the cubs had so far had never been inside a vehicle I was asking a lot of them.

On the 8th of January, about lunch-time, I heard the excited chatter of baboons coming from the bank opposite the studio. This usually meant that the family were around, so later on I went to the studio lugga with my sketch-book. I found Elsa and her sons there and, as they were very sleepy, I had a splendid opportunity of drawing them. Poor Elsa was infested with maggots, but when I had tried to squeeze them out she flattened her ears and growled at me, so I was obliged to leave her alone.

When it got dark and there was still no sign of Little Elsa,

I was anxious, but as her mother did not seem in the least apprehensive I decided not to worry, for I had discovered that Elsa's instinct was more reliable than mine. I am convinced that when there was a source of danger in the neighbourhood she had some means of sensing its presence, and also that she had a way, a quite imperceptible way, of transmitting her wishes to her cubs. We often watched attentively for any indication of a visible or audible sign of communication between her and her children, but were never able to observe one. Yet she was able to make her cubs 'stay put' in the most varied circumstances. She could sense the presence of crocodiles under water, or of hidden beasts which might be a source of danger to her family. She knew when we arrived in camp, even if she were far away at the time, and even if we had been absent for a very long time. She also knew with unerring instinct whether the people she met genuinely liked her or not, and this quite irrespective of their behaviour towards her.

What faculty did she and other highly developed wild animals possess which could account for this? I think perhaps it is the power of telepathy, which we human beings too may have possessed before we developed the capacity to speak.

When I had finished sketching, we all returned to camp, and gave the lions their dinner. After the meal was over, Elsa suddenly got up, listened intently in the direction of the river, and began to walk toward it. I followed at a short distance. We went along the bank for a while, then she turned sharply, crossed the studio lugga, and crept on through the bush till she reached the water's edge. I caught up with her, and in the failing light was just able to see Little Elsa pacing up and down on the far bank, evidently frightened to enter the water, which was fairly deep at this point and where more than once I had seen a large crocodile. Elsa gave her low affectionate moan, moving quickly upstream and keeping her eyes fixed on Little Elsa as she did so. Along the opposite bank, the cub followed her. When they came to a shallow part of the river, Elsa stopped and her call changed, and finally her daughter plucked up enough courage to swim across.

By then it was nearly dark and so as not to add to Little

Elsa's fears, I started to go home. To my surprise, when I emerged from the thick bush, I found Jespah and Gopa apparently waiting for the return of their mother and sister. I took a short cut home so that the family could join up without being disturbed by my presence. Later, Elsa came to my tent and rubbed herself affectionately against me as if to show me how happy she was to have all her family together again and how pleased she was that the anxiety we had shared was over.

But Elsa was to have another alarm before the day was over. While she was still rubbing herself against me, she suddenly stiffened and, her head level with her shoulders, trotted off into the dark. She soon came back, but only to rush off again. She did this several times until she finally settled down to her evening meal with the cubs. Soon afterwards I was startled by the roaring of the cubs' father who can only have been about twenty yards away. I counted the whuffs which followed his roar. There were twelve of them. While this went on, his family stopped eating and stood motionless between him and their dinner; they waited till he had left before they started to eat again. During the night they remained close to the camp, but went off early in the morning and did not return for twenty-four hours. When they came back we gave them some meat, but though the cubs dragged it into the bush they did not eat it; instead, they joined Elsa and myself at the salt-lick.

It was six days since we had placed the lorry by the ramp and, so far as I could judge from the spoor, no lion had been near it. I went into the open truck and called to Elsa; after some hesitation she followed me, but placed herself broadside on to the entrance, thus preventing me from getting out or Jespah, who was following her, from coming in. After a time she went back to the tents and hopped on to the roof of the Land-Rover. The cubs began to eat and I went over to their mother and started to play with her; as I did so, I noticed that two of the maggot swellings had gone septic. I wanted to deal with them, but each time I touched her she withdrew, and when on the following day I again tried to help her she seemed to be even more sensitive.

I always carry a little sulphanilamide powder with me to disinfect insect bites or scratches but George believes that, while they are very effective for human beings, in the case of animals one should not give such drugs unless there is proof that their own antibodies are not strong to effect a natural cure. Because of this, I did not give Elsa sulphanilamide, relying on her natural resistance and thinking that she would lick her wounds clean, as she had often done before when she had been plagued by the maggots.

The lions spent the next day in the kitchen lugga where Nuru and I found them in the afternoon. I sent him off to prepare a carcase at the camp—Elsa managed to keep the cubs away from the goats even though they were developing an increasing interest in them. Had she not always shown such a co-operative attitude our peaceful truce could never have been maintained. On this day, too, she showed her usual tact and sense of fair play when the cubs started to ambush me. All they wanted was a friendly game, but their claws were very sharp. Elsa came to my rescue, cuffed her children, gave me too a mild spanking, and generally saw to it that the cubs' surprise at my reluctance to play with them did not develop into animosity.

There could be no doubt about her wish to maintain good relations between all of us. I had another proof of it on the following afternoon. Nuru and I spotted the lions on the Whuffing Rock. As soon as I called to her, Elsa came and joined us and was most affectionate to me—indeed, she seemed to be making the most of the few moments in which we were alone; as soon as Jespah appeared she became aloof. She was plainly determined not to arouse her cubs' jealousy, was always careful in Jespah's presence, and when Gopa and Little Elsa were about it was an understood thing that no demonstrations of affection were ever to take place between us, for they, more than Jespah, had a tendency to be very jealous of me.

We crossed the thick bush towards the river, and Nuru had a difficult time with Jespah, who took advantage of every piece of cover to pounce out at him and try to get his rifle. It was only because Elsa often stood between her son and him that any progress was possible.

When we reached the river, I told Nuru to take a short cut home and get the lions' dinner ready. He sneaked away as quickly as he could, but Jespah was not going to be deprived of his fun, and stealthily followed him. My 'No's' were without effect; luckily I knew I could rely on Nuru's tactics to get him out of his difficulties. He has a unique way with animals and can always be relied on to be kind to them. How often I have watched him using all sorts of tricks to divert their interest when they were being naughty, rather than resort to force or punishment. In all the years he had been in daily contact with them, he has never once suffered so much as a scratch, and there is no doubt he is genuinely fond of his charges. I would rather have him than anyone else to deal with lions.

While Nuru was making his way home, I took the rest of the family back by the river. When we reached the studio lugga Jespah joined us, and by his spirited prancings I could just imagine what fun he had been having with poor Nuru. When we got to camp the cubs pounced on their dinner and Elsa stepped carefully up on to the roof of the Land-Rover. Her maggot wounds seemed to be hurting her a great deal, but she would not allow me to touch the swellings, much less press the maggots out.

Chapter Two

ELSA IS ILL

GEORGE had now been away for two weeks on the recce to Lake Rudolf. He had been joined by Ken Smith as well as by the game warden for the area. I expected them back any day but almost dreaded to hear the noise of the car, for I feared it might mean the end of Elsa's happy life. What would await her in her new home? How many lionesses might she have to conquer before here territory was safe for the cubs? She loved her home and here she had at least established her rights. She and her children would need to forget this ideal environment and all that was familiar to them before they could begin to be happy in another place. If man with all his capacity to reason often gives tragic proof of his inability to adjust himself to exile, how could one expect wild animals, who are more conservative and more dependent on their territory, to adjust themselves to something completely strange?

Now the lions were in the studio lugga which, flanked by thick bush and overshadowed by large trees, was one of their favourite lie-ups; it provided a cool shelter from the hot sun, soft sand to doze on and usually a slight breeze swept up to it from the river. The family had been there since morning : at tea-time I joined them with my sketch-book. As I drew I listened to the chirping of many birds and the soothing bubbling sound of the river. How peaceful it all was, and how contented we were.

When it got cooler, Elsa woke up, stretched herself, walked over to Jespah and licked him; he rolled on his back and hugged her with his paws. Then she came over to me, rubbed her face against mine and licked me too; afterwards she went over to Gopa and repeated her demonstrations of affection, and then went on to Little Elsa. She had greeted each of us in turn, beginning with the one closest to her and ending with the one farthest away. This was her signal that she thought it time to go home. She started off for camp, looking back every few yards to make sure that we were following. We were not very quick off the mark, for first Jespah wished to investigate all my paraphernalia, and I had only just time to rescue my sketching materials and cameras, put them into bags and hang them on a branch out of his reach. Gopa and Little Elsa had gone ahead, and when I followed they blocked my way so cunningly that there was nothing for me to do but sit down and pretend that I wasn't interested in their antics. It was dusk and the mosquitoes had become very active and rendered my involuntary rest rather disagreeable. Luckily for me, Elsa noticed what was happening and came to my rescue. She cuffed her children playfully, after which they forgot about me and followed her, prodding and chasing each other, which enabled me to make my way home.

That evening, for the first time, I saw Gopa show a sexual impulse, first when playing with Elsa and later with Jespah. It was only play and no doubt he was simply moved by a strange instinct, the significance of which he did not understand. I was surprised that this should happen at such an early age; the cubs were only twelve and a half months old and still had their milk teeth.

During the night I heard the family around the camp, and it was not until after breakfast that they scampered towards the doam-palm logs beyond the salt-lick, where Elsa stood contemplating the lorry. Very soon she stepped cautiously on to the roof of the cabin and sat down. For ten days I had been waiting for her to do just this, but now I felt sad to see her sitting so trustingly on the lorry which was to take her away from her home.

I joined her and tried, without success, to deal with her maggots. She was licking them, and I saw that she had seven swellings, but, as at times she had had as many as fifteen, I was not unduly alarmed.

After a while, the cubs went off to the bush and Elsa followed; in the afternoon they came back and began playing on the logs. Elsa was very impatient with her children, and eventually took refuge on the cabin roof of the lorry to escape their teasing. It would have been easy for them to follow her, but they preferred to make a wide detour whenever they passed the truck.

All that afternoon Elsa rested on the cabin roof, from which she watched her cubs and me. When I went for a short walk she did not follow me, and when I came back I found her still in the same position. After it got dark she came and lay in the grass in front of my tent, but made no attempt to hop on to the roof of the Land-Rover as she usually did. I walked up to her, but was charged by Gopa and Jespah who had been resting nearby in the tall grass.

Early next morning I heard Elsa calling to the cubs in her soft moan, 'Mhm, mhm, mhm'; it was a most comforting sound and always had a very soothing effect on me.

Soon they all disappeared in the direction of the studio lugga; in the afternoon I took a sketch-book and went there. Elsa welcomed me gently and affectionately, and even Gopa showed a sign of friendliness by tilting his head towards me. We spent another lovely afternoon, the cubs playing as I drew. I would have been completely happy but for the apprehension which nagged at me when I thought of the cruel move from which only a miracle could save us. I hoped that Elsa didn't sense my wretchedness and anxiety; she was ill enough as it was with her maggot sores.

When she thought it was time for us to go home she gave us her usual signal by licking each of us in turn. I wondered how long she would be able to maintain the friendly relations which existed between the five of us. For how much longer would I be accepted as a member of the pride? If we suc-ceeded in enabling the cubs to live natural wild lives this would in any case bring the relationship to an end. Our inti-mate life with the lions had only lasted as long as it had be-cause the threat of attack by poachers had compelled us to stay with the family to protect them. On the other hand, if the lions were removed to Lake Rudolf the possibility of their taking up a full wild life would be delayed or even become impracticable. This might be inevitable, but for them to be denied their natural life simply so that I should retain my position as part of the pride was too high a price to pay for my privilege.

Elsa was constantly licking her wounds; I hoped this would help to heal them quickly. That night she again stayed in the grass outside my tent and refused to eat. As I was watching her, Gopa came up to me and wished to make friends. This was unusual, and I wanted to respond, but like Jespah, he had not learned to retract his claws when playing with human beings, so reluctantly I had to disappoint him. I squatted near him, looking him in the face, calling him by his name and hoping that he would understand that even if I would not play with him, all the same I loved him. Jespah brought this awkward situation to an end by bouncing on his brother. The manes of the two lions had grown a lot lately; Gopa's was much darker and nearly twice the length of his brother's; his growl was deep and sometimes threatening. In every way he was a powerful young lion.

Next afternoon I again found the family in the studio lugga. I had brought my sketch-book, but preferred to sit near Elsa and comfort her by stroking her head. She lay quite still and allowed me to pat her, but when I touched her back, or my hand came near one of her sores, she growled and made it very plain that she did not want me to interfere. Her nose was wet and cold; a sure sign that she was ill. Two of the wounds were festering and pus was oozing out of them. I hoped that this meant that they would drain. I still refrained from giving her sulphuanilamide, so as not to weaken her natural resistance, and I was so convinced that the maggots were responsible for her condition that I never thought of taking a blood slide and having it analysed to see whether she had any other infection.

When it got dark, Elsa moved into the bush a few yards from the lugga, and when I left for camp she remained there with the cubs. After waiting for some time to see her appear, I became anxious and began to call her. To my relief she soon came up, walked slowly into my tent and gently licked me.

Afterwards she went out into the dark and I did not see her or the cubs again that evening.

In the morning, I followed their spoor till I saw the lions on top of the Whuffing Rock. As I did not want to disturb them, I painted the rock from a distance until a cloudburst put an end to my efforts.

At tea-time I returned and, through my field-glasses, saw two cubs on the rock. There was no sign of Elsa and, assuming that she and Jespah, though hidden from my view, were close by, I called, but there was no response. The lions did not come to the camp that night. This was not unusual, but I felt worried on account of Elsa's condition, so, at first light I went to the rock. There I was relieved to see all the family on the ridge. I called to Elsa and she raised her head; the cubs didn't move.

At tea-time I went back with Nuru; Elsa at once came out of the bush below the rock, followed by Jespah. She greeted us affectionately, but I noticed that she was breathing heavily and that every movement seemed to require an effort. Jespah acted like a bodyguard and made it difficult for me to stroke her. I sat close to her till Gopa and Little Elsa joined us and then we all started for home. Elsa was very impatient with the cubs and evidently extremely sensitive to being touched. If one of her children brushed against her, she flattened her ears and growled. She did not, however, object to my walking beside her and flicking off the tsetse flies, but got really angry when one of the cubs tried to prod her. I had never before seen her react like this. She sat down repeatedly during the short distance through the bush to the car track, but after we reached the track the going was easier. When we got to the camp she went straight up to the Land-Rover and lay down on the roof very carefully to avoid putting pressure on her sores. She stayed in this position all through the evening. I brought her some marrow, a thing she loved, but she only looked at it and turned away, and when I tried to stroke her paws she moved them out of my reach.

I awoke to hear the cubs chasing each other round the tents, but there was no sign of Elsa. I waited for her familiar moan, but heard only Jespah's high-pitched 'tciang.' I saw him peep through the gate of the enclosure, and as I came out caught sight of Gopa standing on the river bank, about to cross to the far side. When he saw me he gave a startled whuff, plunged in and soon I heard the others greeting him.

Soon it would be four weeks since we had received the deportation order and it was already three since George had gone on his recce to Lake Rudolf. Before he left, we had planned to start the move on the 20th of January; to-day was the 19th; never once had the cubs entered the Thames lorry; the Bedford had not arrived, Elsa was ill, we had not yet found a new home for the cubs or a way of moving them. Plainly, we were going to be far behind our schedule.

Chapter Three

RECCE TO FIND A NEW HOME
FOR THE LIONS

THAT EVENING George arrived, but his news was not good.

He and Ken Smith, driving two Land-Rovers and a lorry, had first gone to Alia Bay, immediately north of the Longendoti Hills. Alia Bay was the place to which we had taken Elsa on the foot safari which I described in *Born Free*. From this range some secluded valleys run down to Lake Rudolf, and it was one of the areas in which George hoped that we might find a suitable home for Elsa and the cubs. Up to now no one had ever reached these valleys by motor, so the first need was to find a possible route. Meanwhile they camped by the lake and were surprised to see large herds of cattle grazing along the shore and even eating weed in the water, thus becoming easy prey for crocodile, with which the lake was infested. The cause of this unexpected assembly of stock was the very severe drought which had forced the Samburu and Rendille tribesmen to venture farther north than they normally do, in search of grazing.

The next morning George and Ken explored the eastern foothills, hoping to find a way through them, but the slopes were precipitous and broken by deep gorges and it would have needed a major engineering feat to make a road through them fit to take the Bedford lorry. Reluctantly, they abandoned the idea of reaching the valleys beyond the foothills.

After travelling some twenty miles over very rough ground, they arrived at a wide, sandy river-bed. George knew that this river entered the lake at the southern end of the hills. The sand was fairly firm, and by driving in low gear with the throttle wide open they made good headway, and were only occasionally held up by drifts of soft sand or by the need to let the engine cool down. The temperature was over 100°F: and there was a fierce following wind, so it was hot work for both the cars and their passengers.

A thin line of trees which grew along the banks of the river bed provided the only shade; beyond them was burning desert. Herds of oryx, grevy-zebra, giraffe, Grant's gazelle and gerenuk were sheltering from the blazing sun in this belt. Many of these animals stared for some time in astonishment at the unprecedented sight of motors and men, before galloping away.

George passed the camping place at which Elsa, after an exhausting march, had attacked our donkeys. By late afternoon they reached Moite, where the river enters the lake and forms a delta. Here they saw very large herds of Grant's gazelle feeding on the coarse, spiky grass and also, to their dismay, a small herd of cattle and goats belonging to the Turkana tribesmen who are not supposed to enter this area. Having got back to the lake, George and Ken flung off their clothes and rushed into the water; they washed the grit off their bodies and lay soaking for an hour.

Next day they explored the country round Moite to see whether it might be a possible home for Elsa and the cubs. On the north side of the delta was an expanse of bush much favoured by hippo, which offered good cover for lions and enough shade to make a reasonably comfortable camp; by the foot of the Moite Hill was a little spring which, if cleaned out, would supply fresh water. There was enough game for the needs of Elsa and the cubs, and a few lions in the area for company and mating. The area was very remote and, as we had supposed, unlikely to become the scene of political complications.

These were the assets; there were also many drawbacks.

To say that the country round Moite is grim is an understatement. It consists solely of sand and lava, is swept by storms, and the sun blazes fiercely down upon it; in fact, it is only made tolerable by the waters of the lake. Moreover, even if Turkana poachers were kept out of the area, it would certainly be visited by Rendille tribesmen and their stock; and these might prove an overwhelming temptation to the lions.

However, since there was a possibility that we might be able to rent sufficient territory in the immediate neighbourhood of Moite for Elsa and the cubs, George felt it would be worth while finding out whether there was any chance of transporting the family to the area. The road by which he and Ken had reached it was impossible for a heavy lorry, so they set off eastwards along a broad ridge which would have made an ideal landing place for even a large aircraft. If, for instance, the R.A.F. were to allow the lions to accompany them on one of the reconnaissance flights, a Beverley transport plane would make the removal of the family to this spot a simple matter. Unfortunately, after a few miles the ridge narrowed and led into broken lava country and George and Ken had to abandon it and take to the sand luggas again. As none of these led in the right direction, they could only follow them for a short distance, and were then obliged to cross a ridge into the next lugga. They had to repeat the process for thirty miles before they got back to the Alia Bay road.

The next reconnaissance was to the north of the bay. After a difficult passage over flooded flats, they reached an opened foreshore with a reasonably firm surface. There they camped on the beach a few yards from the water's edge. George's and Ken's beds were alongside each other, while the four African scouts slept about twenty yards away. George dreamt that Ken was trying to imitate a lion's roar and was reflecting that it was a pretty poor performance and a singularly ill-chosen time to indulge in it, when the roar became so loud that it woke him. He opened his eyes and saw an enormous bull hippo standing a few feet away, its cavernous mouth agape; it was emitting most curious sounds. George wondered what its intentions might be. Suddenly the hippo advanced towards the African scouts. Just as he was about to shout a warning, two shots rang out and the beast turned and plunged into the lake. The scouts had spotted it while George was still asleep; they told him that they had seen it come out of the lake and go towards the place where he and Ken were sleeping. When George inquired why, in this case, they had not fired earlier, they answered that they had not wanted to disturb him unnecessarily.

Next morning, as they were motoring northwards along the shore, George saw people by the water. In this part of Kenya these could only be raiders, poachers or a police patrol. Looking through his field-glasses, he observed that they were naked; this convinced him that they were a party of Galubba tribesmen who had no right to be in the area. He and Ken took them completely by surprise; in their fright they dashed into the lake and, regardless of crocodiles, tried to submerge. But the water was too shallow, so realising that there was no escape they came rather sheepishly ashore again. George soon discovered that they were not, as he imagined, bloodthirsty raiders but a party searching for crocodile eggs. They had already collected a large number, and he decided to leave them to their food, which was simmering in pots over fires.

At last he and Ken came to a place where there were herds of topi numbering several hundred, and besides these, herds of Grant's gazelle, oryx and zebra. In many ways this seemed an ideal spot for Elsa and the cubs to live in; unfortunately, George knew that it was frequently invaded by armed raiders from across the Ethiopian border; this would make it too dangerous for the lions; also, the strict security regulations in force in this area would have prevented my going there.

George had now made a pretty comprehensive recce, and his opinion was that Moite offered the only hope, and this only if he could find or make a passable route to it and get permission to rent some land there.

After overcoming considerable difficulties, the party got back to the lake and camped on the bed of a river called Serrel-Tommia, which means the river of the elephants. Elephants had long ago deserted the place, but George had good reason to remember the place, for twenty-six years earlier he and a friend, optimistically prospecting for gold, had run out of food while camping there. To avoid marching 150 miles on empty stomachs in order to reach Lodwar, the nearest administration post on the far side of the lake, they had built a boat out of tarpaulin stretched over a frame of more or less straight acacia roots. In this craft they had rowed twelve miles across the lake, which is notorious for sudden gales often reaching 90 miles an hour. But luck was on their side and they landed safely before a storm broke.

From Serr-el-Tommia, George and Ken got to Moite without much trouble. It was certainly a better route than the other two they had tried, but that was the most that could be said for it. There were long stretches of soft sand, which would be heavy going for a laden truck, and also several luggas to cross. On their way they passed a few lean, hungry-looking Turkana tribesmen who lived by catching fish and trapping game, and kept a few miserable goats mainly as a respectable screen to their poaching activities.

Before returning to Isiolo, George discussed with the District Commissioner of Marsabit the possibility of renting some land round Moite, and asked for his co-operation in building a 600-mile road and clearing the ground for an airstrip. The District Commissioner gave his consent. We, of course, were to provide the necessary cash. Since the sum involved was considerable, George said he would wait to take a decision until he had discussed the matter with me.

This was the story of his recce.

The prospect of settling the lions near Lake Rudolf seemed very unsatisfactory to me. Even if, by renting land at Moite, we could ensure that they would not be tempted to injure the tribesmen's stock in the area, how could we prevent Elsa and the cubs from leaving this sanctuary? The local lions might object to their presence and what would happen if they were driven into the waterless hinterland? I also feared that once we had built a road it would inevitably be used and, if so, would it not end by evoking the same fears which were the reason for exiling Elsa and the cubs from their present home? For all these reasons I was not at all happy about the prospect of the move to Moite and was much relieved that, in the mail which George had picked up on his way to camp, we found letters from the Rhodesias, Bechuanaland and South Africa in reply to our inquiries, all offering alternative possibilities.

However, since we had no idea whether the ecological conditions in these areas would be suitable for our lions, George suggested that I should go at once to Nairobi and ask the advice of Major Ian Grimwood, our Chief Game Warden, who knew these localities well. If he should consider them unsuitable, then I would telegraph to the District Commissioner at Marsabit asking him to start work at once on the new road and the clearing of a site suitable for an airstrip. George was hopeful that I might be able to arrange to get the loan of a Beverley aircraft, which would be large enough to fly us, the lorry with the lions in it and our camping kit to the lake, while the rest of the safari followed by road. During my absence in Nairobi, he would train the cubs to feed in the Bedford, which was due to arrive, complete with wire enclosure, within a few days.

As there was so little time left, I agreed to go, provided that Elsa was well enough for me to leave her.

That evening we did not see the lions, but we heard them on the far side of the river, so hoped that they were all right. Early next morning we waded to the opposite bank and found the family a few yards from the water. Elsa broke through the dense undergrowth and rubbed herself affectionately against me. I scratched her on the head and behind the ears. Her coat was like velvet and her body hard and strong. I stroked her for a long time, then she greeted George and afterwards Nuru, and finally returned to the bush where her cubs were hiding.

George did not think she looked any worse than she had on earlier occasions when she had been infested with maggots, and this relieved my anxiety. However, as she had not eaten for two days, before I left, we placed meat on the river bank; while we did this Elsa watched us from the far side. As she made no attempt to come over and collect it, George floated it across; he had to put it right in front of her before she rose and, without eating anything herself, dragged it up the steep slope and into the thicket where the cubs were.

With this last picture of Elsa helping her children, I reluctantly left the camp.

On my way to Nairobi I called on the District Commissioner in charge of the area in which the lions were living. I wanted to find out whether there was anything we could do which might result in the rescinding of the deportation order; but he advised me to go ahead with arrangements for the move.

My next visit was to Ken Smith at Isiolo; he was acting for George in his absence. Ken showed me the wire enclosure which had been made to fit the Bedford. It did not seem to me strong enough, so I arranged to have it reinforced.

On my way to Nairobi I called on the veterinary surgeon, John Berger, with whom I had been corresponding about tranquillisers, but though we spent about four hours discussing the problem, we were not able to find a satisfactory solution.

I arrived in Nairobi and went to keep my first appointment which was with the Chief Game Warden, but before we had started our discussion he handed me a telegram from George:

Elsa worse. Has high fever. Suggest bring aureomycin.

Chapter Four

ELSA'S DEATH

THE MESSAGE had been telephoned through from Isiolo by Ken, who had asked Major Grimwood to tell me that he had already sent the drug to George.

I was terribly worried, but since help was already on the way I decided, in view of the urgent need to make arrangements for the move, to stay one night in Nairobi.

Major Grimwood told me that in the homes offered in the Rhodesias and Bechuanaland the ecological conditions would not suit Elsa or the cubs, therefore he advised us to move the lions to Lake Rudolf. He also suggested that the wire enclosure in the lorry had better be partitioned, since, if we transported the family in a communal crate and one lion were to panic, it might hurt the others.

I telegraphed to the District Commissioner at Marsabit asking him to start on the work which George had discussed with him.

Next morning I got up early, as I had some urgent matters to attend to before leaving Nairobi. When I came downstairs I found Ken waiting for me. He looked tired and dusty, having just arrived from Isiolo with a message from George that Elsa was now desperately ill. George had sent an SOS at midnight, asking for me to return and for a vet to come at once. Ken had got in touch with John MacDonald, the vet at Isiolo, who had left immediately, then Ken had driven the one hundred and eighty miles to Nairobi to give me George's message. How grateful I was to him.

I chartered a plane and soon Ken and I were on our way to the small Somali village which was the nearest landing strip to the camp, at which we might be able to hire a car for the rest of our journey. We were lucky enough to find an old Land-Rover and in it drove the last seventy miles.

We arrived at the camp about tea-time, leaving the car some distance away so as not to alarm Elsa. I rushed to the studio. George was sitting there alone, and looked at me without saying anything. His expression told more than I could bear.

When I had recovered from the shock he took me to Elsa's grave.

It was under a tree close to the tents, overlooking the river and the sand-bank where Elsa had introduced me to her children. This was the tree on whose rough bark the cubs had learned to sharpen their claws; under the shade of which the family had so often played and where, last year, Elsa's mate had tried unsuccessfully to get his Christmas dinner.

George told me all that had happened while I was away. This is what he said:

'After you had left I moved my tent near to the ramp and waited for the family to appear, but that night they did not come. In the morning I was obliged to visit a game post higher up the river, so it was not until the afternoon that I was free to look for Elsa. I saw the cubs playing on the far bank, and then found Elsa lying under a bush a little farther up the river. She got up and greeted me and Makedde. The cubs came along and played around their mother.

'I then went back to camp; that night again no lions appeared. Before breakfast I went to look for Elsa; she was lying alone near the place where I had left her the night before. She replied to my calls, but did not get up to greet me. Her breathing was laboured and she seemed to be in pain; she was obviously ill. I returned to camp and at once despatched the Thames truck to Isiolo with the telegram to let you know that Elsa was worse and asking you to send aureomycin. I also sent a letter explaining the situation.

'Then I went back to Elsa with water and a plate of meat and brains into which I had mixed sulphathiazole. She drank a little water but, even in spite of her liking for brains, did not eat anything. I then put some sulphathiazole into the water, but she refused it.

'Then I went back and had lunch; afterwards I returned to Elsa and found that she had moved a little way and was lying in long grass. I felt very much alarmed, for she was steadily growing weaker; she would not look at food, and only drank a little water which I offered her in a basin.

'To leave her alone for the night was unthinkable, for in her weak state she might have been attacked by hyenas, buffalo, or by a lioness. I therefore decided to spend the night with her, and got the boys to bring my bed over from the camp, also the remains of the goat and a pressure lamp. I spent the night in the bush and kept the lamp burning. The cubs came up from the stream and ate the goat; afterwards Jespah tried to pull the blankets off my bed. Elsa seemed to be a little better. Twice she came up to my bed and rubbed her head affectionately against me.

'Once during the night I woke up and found the cubs on the alert looking intently behind my head. Next I heard a loud snort and flashed my torch and a buffalo crashed away into the bush. Elsa lay close to my bed. The cubs were in a playful mood and wanted their mother to join in their game, but every time they came near her she growled.

'At dawn Elsa seemed fairly comfortable, so I went back to camp for breakfast and then did some typing.

'About ten o'clock I began to feel anxious and went to look for Elsa. I could not find her; there was no answer to my calls and no sign of the cubs. For two hours I searched up and down the river and at last I found her lying half in the water by a little island near the camp. She looked desperately ill, her breathing was very fast and she was extremely weak. I tried to give her water in my cupped hands but she could not swallow.

'I stayed with her for an hour. Then Elsa suddenly made an immense effort and went up the steep bank on to the island, where she collapsed. I called Nuru and got him to cut a path to a place from which it was easy to cross the river. Then, I left Nuru in charge, and went back to camp and improvised a stretcher out of my camp-bed and tent poles. When this was ready I carried it back to the island and laid it beside Elsa, hoping that, since she always liked lying on a bed, she might roll on to it. If she did this, I meant, with the help of the men,

to carry her across the river to my tent. But Elsa did not
attempt to get on to the bed. About three o'clock she suddenly rose to her feet and staggered to the river. With my
help she waded across it to the bank below the kitchen. She
was completely exhausted by the effort and lay for a long time
on the bank. At least now she was on our side of the river
and close to the camp. The cubs appeared on the island,
having no doubt followed their mother's scent, but they seemed
nervous of crossing over.

'Stopping twice to rest, Elsa made her way to the sandbank below our tents.

'I showed some meat to the cubs, who followed my progress
along the other side of the river as I dragged their dinner to
the sandbank. Jespah and Little Elsa swam across, but Gopa
hesitated until he saw his brother and sister eating, then he
ventured to swim over and was ambushed by Jespah as soon as
he landed.

'For the next two hours Elsa lay on the sandbank with
Jespah close to her. Twice she got up and went to the water's
edge to drink, but she could not swallow. It was a pathetic
sight. I tried pouring water from my cupped hands into her
mouth but it just dribbled out again. When it got dark she
walked up the narrow path and lay down at the place where
my tent used to stand before I moved it up to the ramp.

'I tried to give her a little milk and whisky by squirting it
into her mouth with a syringe; she managed to swallow
some of it. Then I covered her with a blanket and hoped she
would not move. I was in despair, feeling sure that she would
not last out the night, anxious to send a message to you and
worried because the truck was very much overdue. I realised
that the only hope of saving her was to get a vet as quickly
as possible; on the other hand, I did not want to leave her in
case she wandered off in the darkness, in which case it might
have been impossible to find her.

'In the end, I decided to risk leaving her for an hour and a
half, the time it would take me to go to and from a bad ford
where I thought the truck might be stuck. Less than two
miles from camp I met the truck which had got stuck both

going to and returning from Isiolo. The driver had brought the drug for Elsa. I wrote a letter to Ken, telling him that Elsa was in desperate need of a vet and asked him to get in touch with you. Then I sent the driver straight back to Isiolo in my Land-Rover.

' Fortunately Elsa had not moved. The cubs had arrived and I gave them some meat.

' It was impossible to get Elsa to swallow the drug. She had become very restless, would get up, move a few paces and then lie down again. All my attempts to make her drink failed.

' At about eleven at night she moved into my tent near the studio and lay there for an hour. Then she got up, walked slowly down to the river, waded in and stood there for several minutes making attempts to drink but unable to swallow. Eventually, she returned to my tent and again lay down in it.

' The cubs came to the tent and Jespah nuzzled his mother, but she did not respond.

' At about a quarter to two in the morning, Elsa left the tent and went back to the studio and into the water. I tried to stop her, but she went resolutely on till she reached the sandbank under the trees where she had so often played with the cubs. Here she lay on the sodden mud bank, evidently in great distress, alternately sitting up and lying down, her breathing more laboured than ever.

' I tried to move her back to the dry sand of the studio, but she seemed beyond making any effort. It was a terrible and harrowing sight. It even crossed my mind that I ought to put her out of her misery, but I believed that there was still a chance that you might arrive with a vet in time to help her.

' At about 4.30 I called all the men in camp and with their help put Elsa on the stretcher and with much difficulty carried her back to my tent. She settled down and I lay beside her, completely exhausted.

' As dawn was breaking, she suddenly got up, walked to the front of the tent and collapsed. I held her head in my lap. A few minutes later she sat up, gave a most heart-rending terrible cry and fell over.

' Elsa was dead.'

The cubs were close by, obviously bewildered and distressed. Jespah came up to his mother and licked her face. He seemed frightened, and rejoined the others who were hiding in the bush a few yards away.

Half an hour after Elsa died, John MacDonald, the Senior Veterinary Officer from Isiolo, arrived. Although George hated the idea, he agreed in the interests of medicine and of the cubs themselves, that a post-mortem should be carried out to establish the cause of death.

When this was over, Elsa was buried under the acacia tree where she had often rested (it stands on the river bank, close to the camp); at George's command the game scouts fired three volleys over the grave. The reports echoed back from Elsa's rock; perhaps somewhere in the sea of bush her mate may have heard them and paused.

It was 24th January, 1961.

Chapter Five

GUARDIANS OF ELSA'S CHILDREN

Now we were the guardians of Elsa's children.

Late in the afternoon, we went towards the Big Rock and along the river to look for the cubs. All we found was fresh blood which suggested a large kill close to the studio lugga.

After sunset, I went to the river and sat on the sandbank where, a year ago, Elsa had introduced her cubs to me. I sat there for a long time. Suddenly from the other side of the river, I heard a faint 'tciang.' Instantly I gave all the calls which I hoped the cubs might recognise, and eventually, through the darkness, caught a glimpse of Jespah peeping between the undergrowth; but he vanished as quickly as he appeared.

I placed some meat in the open where the cubs could see it, but they did not come, nor did they give any response to my calls. The only sound I heard was the howling of an unusual number of hyenas. Later, we secured the carcase near George's tent; but the cubs did not come during the night and as we listened to the sinister chorus of hyenas we became very anxious for we did not think that they would stand a chance if they were attacked by such powerful predators.

Next morning, we continued our search. We followed the spoor which Jespah had left on the previous evening. It led upstream, to the place near the island where Elsa had collapsed on the day before she died. We took some meat with us, hoping to tempt the cubs back to camp by giving them only a little at a time, but when we saw Jespah, hiding in a thicket and looking hungrily at the meat, we dropped the whole lot. He grabbed it at once, and ate it ravenously. Then I heard a rustling noise and saw Little Elsa about twenty yards away, but as soon as we looked at each other she bolted.

Haunted by the thought of the many hyenas we had heard

during the night, we wanted to make the cubs stay close to the camp, so we did not provide them with any more food, hoping that hunger would force them to come to us.

Then, as Ken had to return to Isiolo, we went to see him off. When we returned we took out a ration of meat for Little Elsa and Gopa, but when we reached the place where we had left Jespah, he bounced out of a bush and seized the meat before we could stop him. Feeling sorry for Little Elsa and Gopa, who must, I knew, be terribly hungry, we went back and fetched the remains of the carcase. Attracted by it, Gopa appeared. We then dragged the meat towards the camp and were followed by all three cubs, who were obviously very nervous. We floated the carcase over the river, but the cubs remained on the far bank. For two hours they watched us guarding the meat and calling to them, but made no attempt to swim across. So we fastened the carcase to a tree and returned to camp.

During our absence the men had collected three lorry-loads of big stones from the Big Rock. These we piled above Elsa's grave in a large cairn, and cleared the surrounding ground of grass. I wanted to plant a creeper along the base of the cairn, which would in time grow over the pile and hold the stones together. I also intended to plant two candelabra euphorbias at the top and one at the lower end, one to represent each of Elsa's children keeping guard over their mother, leaving an open space round the cairn, about three feet wide. I would set a double row of closely planted aloes to border the gravesite. Finally, I hoped to place a slab of rock on the cairn with Elsa's name engraved on it.

After I had spent an hour helping to arrange the grave, I returned to the cubs and found Jespah and Little Elsa at the meat, but Gopa was still watching from the opposite bank, so I withdrew again and continued helping with the grave.

At dusk, George and I went to see what was happening to the cubs. Jespah and Little Elsa were resting placidly by the meat, but Gopa was still on the far bank. Suspecting that he might come over to defend the 'kill,' George began to drag it towards the camp, but was stopped by Jespah, who pounced on it. We returned to the tents, hoping that Gopa might eventually pluck up courage to come over and get his share.

Later, when we were sitting outside George's tent, which was still pitched close to the ramp, we heard Jespah's 'tciang.' Quickly we told the boys to bring another carcase. When they did so, Jespah stalked them but made no attempt to touch the meat and, as soon as it was placed near the tent, he disappeared. We had left the only chain with which we could secure the carcase at the place where we had seen the cubs during the afternoon, so we went to fetch it, but found both chain and meat gone.

When we got back to camp all three cubs were tearing at the kill, but bolted at our approach. Evidently Jespah had come to reconnoitre and then called his brother and sister to join in the meal. From the moment of Elsa's death he always acted as leader and protector to them. Later, when from downstream we heard the hyenas start up their long-drawn wail, we felt relieved the cubs were near us, but it was only after we had gone to bed that they came back and finished off the carcase.

At dawn I went in search of them and found all three on the Whuffing Rock; though they saw me they did not answer my calls.

Meanwhile, George had gone downstream to look for them. In the rapids in the middle of the river he found the remains of a bull buffalo, obviously the same kill of which we had seen bloody traces two days earlier. Plenty of spoor made by a large lion told of a desperate battle. Yet although this had taken place only some six hundred yards from camp, we had heard nothing except for the aftermath of howling hyenas. The buffalo was a mature bull, which must have weighed at least 1800 lb., and it seemed incredible that a lion scaling not much over 400 lb., could have killed it. George thought it likely that Elsa's mate had been the killer. Vultures were at the remains, and they included three palmnut vultures—an interesting fact, as it is generally believed that these birds do not feed on carrion.

We spent the day working at the grave, and after tea went

to the Whuffing Rock; the cubs were still there, but bolted when we began to climb up to them. We stopped on the ridge which faced the rock but was divided from it by a wide chasm, hoping that this would reassure the cubs. They reappeared and for two hours just sat looking at us without stirring. All our attempts to talk to them were met only by their scrutinising gaze, and I began to feel as though I were on trial for murder. We had to return home alone; and it was long after dark before the cubs arrived. Jespah took immediate possession of the meat and dragged it over to the others who were hiding nearby in a bush.

I went close to them and called softly ' Jespah, Jespah!' He came up to me and allowed me to pat him. I was happy to find myself trusted as I used to be. After this he returned to Little Elsa and Gopa, then I got a stick and, hoping he might play with it, swung it round; he came up and we had a tug-of-war, at the end of which he proudly carried the stick to the other cubs.

They stayed all that night in the camp; whenever I woke up I heard them moving around and also the sardonic laughter of the hyenas at the buffalo kill.

In the morning, George had to go up river to inspect a game scout post. I decided to keep company with the cubs, hoping to gain their confidence by getting them accustomed to my presence during the heat of the day, when they were less active. I found Jespah on the opposite side of the river; he had been dozing under a bush and allowed me to come within a few yards, but watched very alertly every movement I made. After about an hour, he got up and went off. I followed his spoor, which led me to a tree with a large fork which stood on the bank of a deep lugga. Here I caught a glimpse of the other two cubs bolting round a bend.

Suddenly I had a strong feeling that I was being watched. I looked up and saw Jespah sitting in the fork of the tree. He jumped down and ran off to join Gopa and Little Elsa. I stayed for an hour under the tree, so as to give the cubs time to settle down, then I followed and found them at the bend of the lugga, Jespah keeping the rearguard. I approached to within ten yards, then sat down and kept still for another hour, after which I cautiously moved to within three yards of him. Jespah promptly bolted, but when I called to him, he turned, and came very close and looked me straight in the eyes, after which he left the lugga.

It was impossible to see spoor in the long grass, so I walked downstream. Again I had the sensation of being watched and, turning, saw Jespah crouching behind me. I sat down, hoping to encourage him to do the same, but he retreated as quietly as he had approached. I stayed where I was for two hours, and then noticed a slight movement some twenty yards away and immediately afterwards observed two cubs dozing under a bush. None of us moved till tea-time, when George arrived, then the cubs disappeared and we caught a glimpse of Jespah running as fast as he could through the dense bush.

All this made us realise that it was entirely due to Elsa that her cubs had ever tolerated our presence. Since her death, they not only refused to answer our calls, but bolted every time they heard or scented us. So as not to frighten them away from camp by our presence, we placed some meat on the sandbank below our tents, and then went to search for plants for Elsa's grave.

When we were coming back to see how they had got on with their dinner, we heard heavy crashing noises only about three yards away as we walked along the narrow path to the sandbank. We had just missed the old buffalo whose hoof marks I still carry on my thighs. By the light of the torch we saw Jespah on the opposite bank. The cubs had no doubt watched the buffalo, and the incident must have frightened them for they did not come to camp that night.

Early in the morning, we were woken by the excited chatter of baboons coming from the far side of the river, and got up and crossed to the opposite bank to see what it was about. We soon saw the cubs; they were hiding. We had brought two pieces of meat with us, one of which we gave them; the other we held up for them to see and then carried it back to our side of the river, placing it in their view. I spent the whole morning guarding it against vultures, while the cubs watched me but made no attempt to swim over.

At midday, knowing how hungry they must be, I could bear it no longer and floated the meat across. Jespah at once dragged it into a thick cluster of palm-trees. I waded back and, having hidden myself from them, watched the cubs eating voraciously and sometimes going down to the water for a drink. Every time they came into the open they looked round nervously. When the meal was over, I saw Jespah bury the stomach contents and then climb up into a tree. He spent a long time there before joining the others in the bush.

About tea-time, George and I went to have another look; we saw the cubs, but they ran away as we approached. After dark the hyenas began howling from across the river and I felt worried about the cubs, until about midnight I heard their father call. He started from high upstream and gradually came nearer, until I heard him just opposite Elsa's grave. He roared three times, at short intervals. Was he calling Elsa?

It was a clear night, the stars seemed very large and the Southern Cross stood right above Elsa's grave. When their father roared the cubs must have been close to him, for at dawn we found their spoor leading from the camp across the river. We spent all the next day following their pug marks but did not find the cubs; just before dark, at a point far from the camp, we recognised the spoor of the cubs' father and those of the cubs were beside his.

The next day was occupied by a fruitless search, during the course of which we ran into several buffalo and rhino and were charged by a porcupine. In the way of spoor we noticed only those of a single lion, far downstream, and of a lion and lioness up river. We wondered whether these might have been made by the Fierce Lioness and her mate?

In the evening, we tied a carcase to the Land-Rover and hoped the cubs might come to it, but we waited in vain.

It was just a week since Elsa had died. We had expected her children to become dependent upon us, but in fact they had avoided us as far as hunger permitted. Looking back, it seems to me as though there had been a pattern running through Elsa's life of which even her untimely death was a part. While she was alive her stigma of being semi-tame was bound to react upon her cubs and diminish their chances of living a natural life. It was because of their mother that they were to be expelled from their home and obliged to live on the grim shores of Lake Rudolf. Now that she was dead, it seemed possible that they might either be adopted by wild lions and allowed to remain where they were or, if not this, then at least permitted to live in a game reserve or a national park, from both of which Elsa herself would have been banned on account of her friendship with human beings. The cubs were just the right age to adapt themselves to either alternative. I wondered whether Elsa, as so often in the past, had not solved a problem in her own way?

George had to leave the next day for Isiolo. Before he went we made another search for the cubs; as we crossed the river we saw Jespah higher upstream, also crossing. So we gave him a carcase, which he at once floated over to the other cubs, who were hiding on the far bank.

No cubs turned up during the night and all I heard was a lion calling from the direction of the Big Rock.

At dawn I went out with Nuru to look for spoor. We didn't find any, but on our way home heard baboons barking on the other side of the river, and went to investigate. We found Jespah, but only caught a glimpse of Gopa and Little Elsa; all of them seemed very nervous. We fetched some meat and placed it on our side of the river. After an hour, Jespah ventured over, but his brother and sister stayed behind.

I was feeling ill and, when I returned to camp, found that my temperature was 103; I had no choice but to rest till this attack of malaria passed, but, when it grew dark, I got up and collected the remains of the carcase and tied it near my tent.

At about nine I heard the cubs at the meat and saw Jespah standing outside the gate of my thorn enclosure. When I walked up to him his brother and sister bolted.

Worried by the problem of how to regain the trust of the

cubs, who would need our help for at least another ten months, I lay awake that night. It was exactly a year since Elsa had brought them over the river to introduce them to us.

I did not feel well enough to go in search of them again until the following afternoon, then Nuru and I circled the rocks, fruitlessly; on our way home, we tracked a hyena spoor which led to the doam-palm logs near the camp, and there we found the cubs. Jespah followed me back to the tents and allowed me to stroke him while the boys were getting meat for him. When it appeared he pounced on it and dragged it quickly to the other cubs who were hiding. Then, before starting his own meal, he returned to me and placing himself in his 'safe position,' invited me to play with him. He tilted his head and rolled on his back, but as I came up to him made a lightning swipe at me; instantly I jerked back. I had often watched him playfully pressing his sharp claws into his mother's pelt—how could he know that my skin was different? To console him, I rolled an old tyre towards him and offered him a stick, but though he made an attempt to play with these lifeless toys, he soon got bored and went back to the other cubs.

Hoping to find him in a quieter mood after his meal, I waited for a couple of hours and then approached him. Again he gave a quick swipe with his paws which made any further advances on my part impossible. I tried talking softly to Gopa, but he only growled at me and moved off with flattened ears. Jespah followed him, and then placed himself between the two of us, obviously protecting his brother. Suddenly we were interrupted by a snort from the salt-lick. While I collected my torch, Jespah removed the carcase into a thorn thicket.

Although so young, and himself in need of help, he was proving a responsible leader of the pride, always ready to care for his brother and sister.

The cubs did not reappear for two days. One evening I heard Jespah's 'tciang,' and as a boy carried some meat towards the tent he bounded out of a bush and disappeared with it as quickly as he had appeared. Later I heard a lion calling from the Big Rock and next morning found the cubs' pug marks leading in the opposite direction.

At tea-time George arrived from Isiolo.

We had now received the result of Elsa's post-mortem. She had died of an infection by a tick-borne parasite called babesia, which destroys the red blood corpuscles. The four per cent infection which they found had proved fatal because of the weak condition to which she had been reduced by the bites of the mango flies.

It was the first time that such an infection had been found in a lion.

Chapter Six

PLANS TO MOVE THE CUBS

ON THE day of George's return the cubs only came into camp after dark, Jespah first, followed later by Gopa and Little Elsa. Again Jespah invited me to play with him, and now that George was back I felt that I could risk a scratch, so, overcoming my fear, I held my hand out. Before I knew what was happening Jespah tore open one of my finger joints. It was not a serious wound, but it was bad enough to make me realise sadly that we two could never play together.

George brought news that Major Grimwood would be passing through Isiolo the next day, so I decided to meet him there, since we wanted to discuss the cubs' future with him. If it were necessary to move them we hoped that he would help us find a home for them in an East African game reserve.

Major Grimwood proved most sympathetic, and promised to contact the authorities of the National Parks of Kenya and Tanganyika.

I brought an old crate back to camp with me. It had originally been made to take Elsa to Holland. Now I hoped to induce the cubs to feed inside it.

This was our plan : the cubs must get accustomed to feeding in the large communal crate, placed on the ground. Then, one day, when all three were inside, we would close the door and, disguising the tranquilliser in marrow, we would administer a dose in each of the three pie-dishes. We would push the dishes through a second door, small enough to prevent the cubs from escaping through it. The cubs would be safe inside the crate during the time the drug was taking effect. This was important, for we didn't want them to wander about in a state of semi-unconsciousness and perhaps become a prey to predators. As soon as they had been immobilised by the

53

drug, we intended to transfer them to three separate crates, specially designed to fit the back of a five-ton lorry.

I arrived about midnight and found all the cubs guarding their meat close to the tents. They did not mind the glare of the headlights, even when I turned them in their direction. We had noticed that though they were so nervous during the day, they showed little apprehension when it was dark. George had to return next morning to Isiolo, so I once more found myself in charge of the camp. I always slept inside my Land-Rover when I was alone, and parked it close to the meat as a guard against predators.

On the evening of the 10th of February, I was very happy to see the cubs chasing each other round the tents after their evening meal, for they had been distressingly subdued since their mother's death, and up to now had kept quiet after eating, just sitting still and watching.

Next evening I placed the crate in position and secured the meat near to it. When the cubs arrived at their usual time, Jespah, after a few suspicious sniffs, went into the crate. Then he came out and settled down near the meat with Gopa and Little Elsa. I talked to them in a low voice, hoping they would gradually learn to associate food with my presence. I now prepared three pie-dishes every day, filling each dish with a mixture of codliver oil, brain and marrow, hoping in this way to train the cubs to eat separately, so that when the time came to give them tranquillisers they would each get their ration of the drug, concealed in the titbits, and avoid the risk of any of them getting an overdose.

During the next three days, the lions kept to their routine —spending the days across the river, at the place where they had last been with their mother, and coming into camp after dark for their dinner. I did not interfere with their routine in any way, hoping that this would reassure them and make them trust me. I felt that I was succeeding when one evening Jespah crossed the river very early, about six, and licked the pie-dish clean while I was holding it in my hand. Whenever I said the word Elsa—which I did every time I called her daughter—

Jespah looked up very alertly. He and Gopa knew their own names very well. That their sister should share their mother's name was confusing, but I felt that they must get used to it. In case of an emergency it was essential that Little Elsa should know that I was calling her.

After a peaceful evening together I retired into the Land-Rover. At about three o'clock in the morning I heard the cubs' father calling in a low voice from across the river. It sounded as though he were talking to the cubs. Thinking that they might have crossed the river, and wishing to save the meat from predators, I struggled out of the car to fasten it inside the crate. But I was very sleepy, and fell over a sharp tree-stump and split my shin open; blood poured out of the wound, so much indeed that I hoped it had cleaned the wound of any possible infection from the old meat which had been left on the stump. I dressed the wound as well as I could by the light of my torch, and went back to bed, but the pain kept me awake all night. I heard the cubs' father calling again from the Big Rock, and in the morning Nuru told me that he had found the cubs' pug marks leading to the rock.

I had to keep my leg up all morning to prevent it from bleeding; I had already lost a lot of blood and felt quite dizzy. By the afternoon I felt better and was able to go out with Nuru to examine the pug marks and saw that those of the cubs soon joined up with their father's spoor. I did not want to disturb them, so came back and watched two parrots until it became dark.

Jespah arrived about 8 p.m. and was soon followed by the other cubs; until the early hours of the morning I watched them eating and playing. The pain in my leg kept me awake, and I lay wondering whether their father was ever going to feed his cubs or teach them to hunt.

George's return on the following day coincided with Jespah's first meal inside the crate. Gopa and Little Elsa watched him but showed no desire to emulate him. However, after we had gone to bed, they plucked up courage and both ventured into the crate to get their dinner. This was a great relief to us. Now that we knew that they were able to over-come their fear of this strange object, we felt that we must at once order the kind of crates in which they could be moved.

Usually wild animals are moved to zoos in wooden crates with solid walls on three sides; and these do in fact prevent the animals from doing themselves any serious physical injury. We had, however, witnessed the removal in these conditions of three wild lions which were to be released into game reserves and when they arrived at the release point they had been in such a state of panic that they ran amok and had to be shot.

To minimise the risk of panic, we decided to have three sides of the crates made of iron bars, so that during the journey the cubs would be able to see each other and, with-out being able to do any harm, could give each other moral support. There was, of course, a greater risk that they might get chafed against the bars, but we felt that this physical damage would heal more easily than a mind which had been injured by terror. The fourth side of the crates was to consist of a wooden trap door.

Having made up our minds about this, I set off to Nanyuki, two hundred and twenty miles away, to order the three travel-ling crates. On the way home I passed through Isiolo, where I found a message from a pharmaceutical firm offering to supply medicine which might help the cubs to overcome their present state of anxiety. Since Elsa's death we had received many letters of sympathy, letters which proved how well she had been loved by people all over the world; various officials connected with zoos had suggested taking the cubs, but this was the first practical offer which took their immediate con-dition into account. I waited in Isiolo until I could meet the representatives of the firm and was much touched by their gift of the antibiotic terramycin in powder form which they be-lieved would strengthen the resistance of the cubs.

I was also extremely grateful for their advice on tranquil-lisers. Our inquiries had suggested that Librium was the only one which we could risk giving the cubs. Lions are not only highly sensitive to drugs, but are also apt to react to them individually, and therefore unpredictably. Librium, however, has so wide a safety margin that even if one cub accidentally got two doses, it was unlikely to suffer any serious ill effects. The disadvantage of Librium was that we should have to conceal as many as 80 10-milligram capsules in lumps of meat, and I was doubtful whether the cubs would consent to swallow such a quantity. My new friends now suggested that I should write to the manufacturers and ask them to make up capsules with a dose sufficiently concentrated to reduce the number we should need to give from 80 to 4. I wrote at once. Unfortunately, it proved impossible to make such a concentrated capsule.

When I got back to camp, George told me that he had had an exciting time while I was away. On the first day the cubs had come in in the late afternoon and, though a lion had called, they had remained by the tent all night. On the following afternoon, he had followed their spoor to the Whuffing Rock, climbed up it and called to them. Finally, Jespah had appeared, sat down near him and allowed George to scratch his head. Then Little Elsa came into view, but remained some distance away; as for Gopa, all he saw of him were the tips of his ears, sticking up behind a rock.

On the way home, George put up three buffalo and one rhino, and was glad that the cubs were not with him. After dark they came into camp and fed off some meat which was chained outside the crate, until Jespah dragged it inside. After this meal the cubs crossed the river and spent the next twenty-four hours playing on the other side. George saw them climbing trees and noticed that they managed to get quite high up. They didn't come in that evening for a meal, so next morning Nuru took the uneaten meat towards the studio, intending to hang it up in his cool bush-fridge there. As he was climbing down the tree, Jespah jumped at the meat and narrowly missed him. Soon afterwards, George arrived and saw Jespah tearing at the hanging meat watched by Little Elsa from the branch of a tamarind tree on the far bank. When Jespah went to have a drink George took the opportunity to cut the meat down; on his return Jespah dragged it to the river and floated it across to his brother and sister.

About tea-time George surprised the cubs on a sandbank. Gopa and Little Elsa bolted, and were followed by Jespah. An hour later he waded over and spent twenty minutes calling to the cubs without getting any response, then he noticed a movement high up in the tamarind tree and looking up, saw a leopard perched on one of the top branches; it was busy eating the remains of the meat it had stolen from the cubs.

Jespah now appeared and started to climb up towards the leopard, who spat and snarled at him. As the thinner top branches were too weak to sustain the cub's weight, Jespah found himself obliged to settle in a fork near the ground.

To get a better view, George began to climb up the bank; at this moment the leopard sprang down, passing within a few feet of Jespah. After landing, he made off as fast as he could, with all three cubs in pursuit. George followed their spoor down river until he came upon Jespah, who was looking intently at the tree-tops around him; but as George could not see any sign of the leopard he decided to leave him and return home.

Long after dark the cubs came into camp and Jespah took his cod-liver oil from a pie-dish which George held out to him. Gopa ate his dinner inside the crate. I had arrived by then, and was glad to see that he was getting used to the idea of eating it there.

We were both very proud of Jespah: leopards and lions are natural enemies. Of course a leopard would stand no chance against a fully grown lion and so would give way to it; but for a young cub to tackle a leopard was quite another matter, and Jespah had shown great pluck in the encounter.

I was woken in the morning by soft moans that sounded very familiar—indeed, I could hardly believe that it was not Elsa calling. But in fact it was Jespah telling his brother and sister to stop their morning chase round the tents and follow him over the river. Not long afterwards I heard all three splashing across; and then two lions roaring upstream.

Very late that night Jespah appeared for a brief moment : evidently he had come as a scout to make sure that all was safe, for soon he returned with Gopa and Little Elsa. He took the cod-liver oil and let me pat him on the head, muzzle and ears, standing quite still as I did so. After the lights were out George saw Little Elsa join her two brothers in the crate which, with the three cubs and the 'kill' inside it was rather crowded.

On the following day I again found myself in charge, as George had to leave for Isiolo. In the afternoon, when I saw the cubs on a sandbank near the studio, I observed that Gopa's mane was now very well defined. It was about two inches longer and much darker than Jespah's blond ruff.

All I heard that night were heavy splashings, which sounded like buffalo in the river, and there was no sign of the cubs until the following evening. They were all very hungry, and Little Elsa cuffed her brothers and made it quite plain that she did not intend to be deprived of her share of the cod-liver oil which as a rule they licked up before she had a chance to get near it.

Suddenly I heard snorting coming from the river bush and also heavy thuds which suggested the presence of a large animal. The cubs listened for a second, and then went off to investigate and give chase. I was very relieved when they came back to finish their meal. Much later I heard a hyena wailing from the direction of the studio; it sounded as though the animal were in pain. Next morning I found the spoor of a rhino, which was certainly the animal the cubs had chased away, and also the pug marks of a lion in the studio.

Again it was after dark before the cubs came into the camp. This time the brothers showed very good manners and waited to allow Little Elsa to have her cod-liver oil before taking their share. They all still found difficulty in opening a carcase, and as the boys had forgotten to do so that day I waited my opportunity and then went to the cub's assistance. When Jespah saw me interfering with their 'kill' he charged me. The situation was tricky for a moment as the carcase and I were inside the crate and the cub blocked the exit. Luckily he seemed to realise that I was trying to help them, and waited till I had finished the job; in this he gave proof of a degree of intelligence and good nature which reminded me very much of his mother.

More than twenty-four hours passed before I saw the cubs again; then in the early hours of the morning I heard their father's call, first from close by, and finally from near the Big Rock; and soon afterwards I heard the cubs lapping water out of the steel helmet which was still their favourite drinking bowl. I climbed out of the car to open the crate and give them access to their dinner, but they paid no attention to me and walked off determinedly towards Big Rock, obviously more interested in joining their father than in having a meal. Was he, I wondered, perhaps helping to provide food for them? During the rest of the night I heard repeated whuffings from the rock, and next morning found the spoor of all the lions leading to it. To my disappointment, by next evening their father had deserted the cubs again; I heard him roaming round, and they came into camp very hungry. In spite of this they waited patiently for me to open the crate and rushed at the meat after I had got inside my 'sleeper.' They finished every scrap I had prepared for them before crossing the river at dawn. I lay awake all night; my leg was very painful and I kept worrying about the cub's future. We had still no reply to the inquiries which Major Grimwood had kindly made into the possibilities of finding an asylum for them in an East African reserve. I wondered whether, if the cubs joined up with their father, they might not be allowed to remain here in their own home? But as I could do nothing to contribute to either of these solutions, my job for the present consisted in keeping the cubs in good health until some answer to the problem offered itself.

Chapter Seven

HAVE THE CUBS FOUND A PRIDE?

RAMADHAN had now begun, and towards sunset our devout Mohammedan staff chanted prayers so loudly that I wondered whether the cubs would not be too frightened by this unusual sound to come into camp. During this fasting period I could expect little help from our boys, and was therefore much relieved when George returned. The cubs came in after dark, and Little Elsa was more than ever determined to get her share of cod-liver oil before her greedy brothers finished it all up. We always kept large quantities of it in the camp, and the fact that the cubs all liked it now proved very convenient, for we had up to now not been able to make them swallow the terramycin.

This evening, for the first time, the cubs rested near Elsa's grave. It was a month since it had been made, but although it used to be their favourite playground we had never seen them there or found their pug marks near it since their mother's death.

This may have been coincidence, or due to the strong sense of smell that lions possess. On the other hand, there is evidence which suggests that animals with a highly developed intelligence appear to have some conception of death.

This is particularly true of elephants. There was, for instance, an elephant who was apparently highly esteemed by his companions. When he died of natural causes three bull elephants stayed by the body for several days, then drew out the tusks and deposited them a little distance away from the body. Another curious occurrence took place when George was obliged to kill an elephant which had become dangerous. He shot it at night in a garden at Isiolo. Next day the carcase was moved because of the smell. On the following morning he found that the shoulder blade of the dead animal had been

brought back by his companions and laid on the exact spot at
which he had been killed.

We have also come across several instances in which
elephants appeared to be concerned about the death of a
human being.

On one of our safaris we were told by the local tribesmen
that a man had been killed a few days earlier by an elephant
and that since then the animal had come each afternoon to
stand for an hour or two over the place where the tragedy had
occurred. We investigated the facts and they appeared to be
true.

On the 27th of February we found the cubs on the top of
the Whuffing Rock resting in the shade of some candelabra
euphorbias. Jespah came when we called to him, sat close
to me and tilted his head, but kept his eyes fixed on Gopa
and his sister. After a time Little Elsa came a little nearer
to us, but Gopa kept aloof and behaved as though we did not
exist. I saw an unusually large tick on Jespah and I was
alarmed, fearing that it might carry babesia, but however cunningly I tried to remove the parasite he prevented me and
interpreted my actions as an invitation to a game. It was a
lovely afternoon, peaceful and timeless; everything around
us held memories of Elsa, and how like her Jespah was, with
his intelligent expression and friendly, responsible nature.
We took many photographs and only went home after the
sun had turned a deep red.

As soon as we had come down from the rock Gopa and
Little Elsa joined Jespah, and all stood silhouetted against
the sunset. They seemed to be watching us intently, but perhaps they were really watching the buffalo who broke cover
from the base of the rock as soon as we came near it and
crashed past within a few feet of us, fortunately as anxious
to avoid an encounter as we were. The cubs remained standing on the top of the rock until finally we were unable to
make them out in the fading light.

During the next two nights the cubs stayed away from camp.
After hearing a lion calling from the far side of the river,
George followed their spoor, discovered that they had drunk

at the point where the river comes nearest to the Whuffing Rock, and that after drinking they had crossed to the other side. The next day he found their pug marks about two miles downstream, close to those of a lion and lioness. All led to the rocky ridge to which Makedde had traced Elsa's spoor last July, after she had been absent for sixteen days.

George circled the ridge and observed that the cubs' spoor stopped at one end of the rocks, while the pug marks of the lion and lioness stopped at the other.

I could not join George in these searches, for the state of my leg made walking impossible. It was three weeks since I had cut open my shin on the tree-stump. At first the wound seemed to be healing, but then it got worse and by now it looked alarming and was very painful. I had tried to doctor it myself, but by now it was obvious that I must get professional advice.

Knowing that George would only be able to spend a few days in camp, I decided against going to the nearest European hospital which was two hundred miles away, but to seek help from the mission hospital in the nearby hills, even though it was only for African patients and did not normally offer accommodation to other races.

I set off with Ibrahim very early in the morning and, after an extremely bumpy drive, we arrived at the mission at midday. As soon as the doctor saw my wound, he took me straight to the operating theatre. When I came round from the anaesthetic, I found myself in the Matron's office, where she had very kindly rigged up a bed for me. She told me that they had had to cut out a piece of flesh the size of an egg. She and the doctor looked after me with great kindness for two days, and by then I had recovered sufficiently to return to camp. Ibrahim had come to the mission each day with notes from George giving me news of his search for the cubs.

2nd March. Little news. Found only old spoor, some two miles downstream, and excrements containing buffalo hair. So either the cubs have been eating a buffalo killed by their father, or they found a dead one, probably killed by rinderpest, of which there are a lot about. During my afternoon search, found the tracks of three poachers or honey hunters crossing my morning spoor. It seems almost certain that the cubs have joined up with one or more lions down river, a long way below the cataract. I do not expect them back to-night. This is obviously their great adventure. Perhaps by now they are part of a new pride with their father and a stepmother.

I don't think you need worry unduly about them. They know the country well and are capable of finding their way back to camp if they want to; but for the moment I expect they are far too excited to think of the good meal waiting for them in camp—that will come later.

3rd March. The cubs did not turn up during the night. Set off about 7 a.m. this morning down river on the far bank. Saw no fresh spoor until Nuru and I got to the crossing below cataract. There I sent Nuru over to see whether there was anything on the other side. He found only old spoor. Told him to look a little farther. Presently he reappeared and beckoned to me. I crossed over and saw all three cubs— apparently they had just arrived from down river. Jespah came up and sat close to us while the others hid in the bush. We started back towards camp and after going a few hundred yards, stopped and waited for the cubs. Jespah appeared. But as it was the heat of the day I thought the cubs would lie up in the thick undergrowth. I returned to camp, arriving there about 11.30 a.m. About an hour later I heard baboons barking down river. In the afternoon I walked to the Hyrax Rock and found all three cubs sitting on top of it. Took several colour stills and then made my way back to camp, to find that Ibrahim had arrived with news of your operation. He told me that at about 5 p.m. just after crossing the small river between here and the hospital, he saw a big lion and three cubs sitting beside the road. Two of the cubs were male and one female— the same age as Elsa's cubs. Naturally Ibrahim thought they were hers, together with their father. He stopped the car a few yards away from them. The lion and two cubs moved away a short distance; the third cub sat still beside the road.

Elsa and Jespah, January 1961

George and Makedde pull a young crocodile they have killed from the river

Getting accustomed to the lorry

Jespah, Gopa and Little Elsa just after their first birthday

Elsa crosses the river with her cubs

Jespah in January. His mane is beginning to grow

The last photograph of Elsa with Joy (taken by Peter Saw)

Elsa's grave

The cubs kept their distance after Elsa died

Joy with Jespah, February 1961

Ibrahim called 'Jespah, Jespah! Cu-cu-ooo!' The cub tilted its head. Ibrahim opened the door and half got out—still the cub sat. Meanwhile the rest of them reappeared and sat down on the other side of the car. Is it not an extraordinary co-incidence? If it were not for seeing our cubs this afternoon, I would have been convinced that he had seen Elsa's children and would have driven at once to this river. It is almost un-canny. Is it possible that Ibrahim's Ramadhan fasting has proved too much and he is suffering from hallucinations?

The cubs appeared about 7.30 p.m. not at all hungry, and up to now—9.30 p.m.—have scarcely eaten anything, though Jespah promptly came up demanding his brain and cod-liver oil and took them out of my hand. They stayed all night, left about 5 a.m. and have gone towards Whuffing Rock. Heard two more lions calling up river.

4th March. About 5 p.m. I went to the top of the Whuffing Rock and found the cubs there. Little Elsa was the only one who came out and sat about forty feet from me until sundown. I returned to camp. By 11 p.m. cubs had not arrived, so went to bed. 12.30 a.m. I woke up to find Jespah in my tent. Got up and gave him cod-liver oil and brain, and other cubs ate goat inside the crate. Went back to bed. About 1.30 a.m. was aroused by a startled 'Whuff-whuff' from one of the cubs—a sure sign that other lions were in camp. As I got up, heard growls and squabbling in the nearby bush—then full-throated roars of two lions a few yards away. They roared for a long time in and around camp, until one of them went to the studio, calling in a low tone, and then back along the track to-wards the kitchen lugga. Afterwards I heard a single moan which sounded like a cub from near the kitchen. A few minutes later the lions were back in camp, and after more roaring I heard them finally splashing through the river and their roars receded downstream.

5th March. At dawn found lion spoor all round the camp and through it. One lot of lions had crossed over the river on to our side at the kitchen crossing—probably these were our cubs when they came into camp. One lion has come from the direction of the kitchen lugga, and another through the bush between the kitchen lugga and the road. Two had crossed over to opposite bank below the buffalo-path—again probably the cubs—and two or three had crossed at the point where the goat carcase is hung up. The lions had apparently chased each other on the sandbank where Elsa lay at the time of her death. I followed up the spoor of two cubs on opposite side of river up the ridge towards the Shamba Rock. Lost it and came on the tracks of a big lion going up a gully. Near the rocks where Elsa used to lie I found the spoor of a lioness and cub.

There are two alternatives: the cubs panicked when lions appeared and bolted across river, or they joined up and have gone off with them. The fact that the cubs did not appear in camp until 12.30 a.m. and that they might have come across the river would suggest that they had been with the lions before coming into camp, and that later the lions followed them.

George had to leave for Isiolo on the 25th of March, the day I returned from hospital. That night no cubs appeared and I did not know whether to be pleased or worried. If they had joined up with a pride and were being taught to hunt by a lioness, then they would go wild before the question of deporting them arose; and this would probably be the best thing that could happen to them. On the other hand, they might have been driven away from the camp by the wild lions and be in desperate need of help.

The state of my leg made it quite impossible for me to try to follow up their spoor. So I tried to make the best of my handicap by telling myself that it would at least prevent me from interfering, and that this was a good thing because if the cubs had been adopted by a pride any disturbance might cause their foster-parents to abandon them. Still, I did not *know* that they had joined up with a pride and the uncertainty was distressing.

The next day again passed without the cubs putting in an appearance. In the evening, sitting in my tent and straining my ears for the faintest sound, I suddenly felt something soft touch my foot. It was a tiny bird, no doubt seeking refuge from a mongoose, which appeared immediately afterwards at the entrance of my tent. I picked up the frightened little creature and kept it until the mongoose had disappeared, then I released it. During the night I heard lions roaring repeatedly from across the river. The calls sounded immature and ended with only four or five whuffings. I wondered if they were made by our cubs.

In the morning I found that the mongoose must have returned after I had gone to bed and eaten the marrow I had prepared for the cubs.

Nuru and Makedde spent the next day tracking, but found no fresh spoor. In the early hours of the following morning I heard several lions roar, accompanied by the shrieking of baboons upstream. It seemed as though the lions were rapidly approaching the camp, for the roars came from nearby and grew louder, until suddenly they stopped. I lay awake listening, but heard no lion calls until two hours later, when they came from far upstream. When I got up I was surprised to see the pug marks of a lion and a lioness right up beside the car I had been sleeping in. The men went off tracking, but saw no sign of the cubs, though across the river they found the spoor of two lions.

Another day and night passed without news of the cubs before George returned. He made a fruitless search that afternoon. Next morning he and Nuru set out again. Beyond the cataract they found the cubs' spoor coming from the elephant lugga down to the water and back again. The pug marks turned into running tracks, which suggested that the cubs had heard or scented their pursuers.

While he was examining the spoor George was startled by a lion roaring quite close to him in the direction he had just come from. Thinking that it might be the cubs' father calling to them, George and Nuru hid and waited expecting them to return or their father to appear and go to join them; but nothing happened, so in the end, hot and thirsty, George and Nuru returned to camp. Later they went back to the same place and found that the cubs in the meantime had joined up with a young lion or lioness close to where George had been hiding. Now he observed vultures circling nearby, but it was getting dark so he had to postpone his investigation till the next day.

All night I listened to a single lion roaring on the Big Rock. Early in the morning George went spoor tracking while I drove to hospital to have my leg dressed. When I returned George told me that he and Nuru had put up at least four lions below the cataract. As they were bolting, Nuru caught sight of a cub which he felt convinced was Jespah. The running spoor seemed to confirm this, as among them were the pug marks of three cubs. George waited, hoping that at least Jespah might return; then, after an hour, he followed the tracks and found a place where a cub had evidently been lying down only a few minutes earlier. Feeling sure now that the cubs had been adopted by a pride, George did not pursue them for fear of upsetting the foster-parents.

Most nights now we heard two lions roaring round the camp: George thought he recognised their calls as those of the Fierce Lioness, who had attacked Elsa, and her mate. We believed that this pair was not part of the pride which had apparently adopted Elsa's cubs.

During the next few days, George found the spoor of at least five lions, of which three were cubs. It seemed that this pride always stayed between the cataracts and the elephant lugga. This would, we thought, be an ideal home for our cubs; there was plenty of game and comparative safety from poachers.

As George could never get a view of the lions during the day-time, he spent one night near their tracks inside the Land-Rover, but had no luck.

We could not be certain but we began to believe that the cubs had themselves solved the problem of their future, for we had not seen them for twelve days.

Chapter Eight

THE CUBS IN TROUBLE

ON THE 16th of March George and Nuru left early for their daily search.

I was alone in camp when two Game Scouts and an informer arrived to report that during the night of the 13th/14th three lions had attacked the bomas of tribesmen on the Tana River and mauled four cows. The Africans had tried to drive them away with stones, fire and wooden clubs, but they had persistently returned. They believed that the raiders were Elsa's cubs and they begged George to come and dispose of them.

I immediately sent the men to contact George, which they eventually did by firing shots. They all returned to camp and after lunch set off for the scene of the raids. As the crow flies, the distance was only about fifteen miles, but for us there were only two alternatives : either to drive the Land-Rover, as though it were a tank, through forty-five miles of dense bush, or to make a detour of a hundred and twenty miles along a very rough road and walk the last eight miles. George decided to go through the bush.

After loading up the car with camp kit and two goats, he crossed the river with considerable difficulty and disappeared into the bush on the opposite bank. What happened after that he told me when we met again.

When dark fell he was still four miles from his objective, so he spent the night in the bush and next morning abandoned the car and walked to the village.

In all there were eight bomas within a short distance of each other; they consisted of groups of small circular mud huts protected by a shoulder-high thorn fence some six foot wide. The country surrounding the bomas was dense bush, which meant that a lion could approach the huts without being

69

seen. The bomas were close to the River Tana, where the tribesmen watered their stock.

The tribesmen confirmed that during the night of the 13th/14th three lions had mauled two cows before they were driven off, that on the following night (14th/15th) they had mauled two more before being chased away, and that on the third night (15th/16th) they had killed two cows at a different boma from the one they had previously raided, and had eaten one of them within three hundred yards of the hut.

George saw the spoor of a lioness; she had entered an almost impenetrable thorn enclosure and then forced her way out of it. He then tried to examine other lion spoor, but had difficulty in doing so as most of the pug marks were obliterated by cattle tracks. However, he managed to trace the lions back to the place on the river bank where they had drunk. He continued down river expecting to find fresh spoor where they had probably drunk during the preceding night, and was not disappointed, for he came upon new pug marks made by three lions.

With two scouts and a guide he took up this spoor. About an hour later they were casting about in a dry watercourse covered with thick vegetation when suddenly about ten feet away he saw a lioness lying asleep, partly concealed by the trunk of a tree. He watched her for several minutes; she looked like a mature lioness. A scout who was a few paces behind signalled to George and tapped his rifle. He looked at it and found that he had forgotten to load it. Even the clatter of the bolt as he loaded it failed to wake the sleeping animal. In a whisper the scout urged George to shoot, saying that it was a full-grown lioness. It would have been very easy to put a bullet into her brain. But something made George hesitate. Suddenly, the lioness sat up and looked straight into his eyes. She wrinkled her face into a snarl, and, giving a low growl, dashed off. Simultaneously, he heard two other lions break away. He felt convinced that these were not our cubs, but was glad all the same that he had not fired, for how could he be quite certain? He called the cubs by name, but there was no response. Facts which helped to strengthen his belief that these raids were not the work of our cubs were the cunning manner in which the lions had attacked the village and forced their way through the particularly strong thorn fence, and also the apparent ease with which the two fully grown cows had been killed. All this suggested the work of experienced lions.

George told the tribesmen to report any further raids immediately, and then returned to camp.

Discussing the circumstances of the raids together, we came to the conclusion that it was so improbable that Elsa's cubs would be involved that we decided to take up the search again in our own area.

On the following morning George and Nuru, walking along the river bank, met a party of honey hunters. These men hang hollowed section of tree-trunks, which look like barrels, on the boughs of trees frequented by bees. After a swarm has occupied this prefabricated hive, the honey hunters wait until the bees have produced their honey and then smoke them out and take their store. Honey is often the only form of sugar known to primitive tribesmen. A gentlemen's agreement exists between honey hunters by which they respect one another's hives and they risk severe punishment if they steal from another honey hunter. The hives can be identified by the owner's individual mark which he engraves on his barrels. We have often been presented with a sticky mass taken straight from one of these hives. Boiled down and strained, it produces pure honey and if the bees have been feeding on acacia flowers has a particularly delicious taste. Unfortunately the honey hunters are often responsible for devastating bush fires, which they start through carelessness.

On this occasion the honey hunters proved informative and helpful. They told George they had seen the spoor of five lions at a drinking place higher upstream. He went off in this direction and, near the mouth of the elephant lugga, saw two cubs resting on an island in the river; but they bolted before he could focus his field-glasses. Simultaneously, he heard more lions breaking away. Following their spoor, he came upon the carcase of a young buffalo which must have been killed the night before. Five lions had feasted on it. George felt sure these must have been Elsa's cubs and their foster-parents. He called to Jespah, and went on doing so for a long time, and thought he heard a faint moan from the far side of the river, but no cub came in sight, so he returned to camp.

As it was likely that the lions would go back to the buffalo kill, George set off next morning in the Land-Rover, intending to spend the night near it. He devoted the day to tracking and discovered that the lions had moved up to the elephant lugga. He and the two scouts spent the night in the dry river bed, under a high bank which was the safest place he could find. No lions appeared, but a terrible thunder-storm drenched the poor men to the skin and washed away all spoor.

Lying awake in my tent, I heard a lion roaring upstream and later the heavy breathing of an animal near the goat truck. Then the cloudburst reached me, and made spooring impossible.

When George returned from his night on the river bed, he had to go at once to Isiolo to attend to some court cases.

All through the next night the downpour continued, and by the morning the river was only just fordable. Nevertheless, an informer managed to get across. He brought a message from the headman of the Tana settlement stating that their stock had again been raided by lions.

I sent Ibrahim to Isiolo to tell George the news. The next day Ibrahim came back with the message that George would go to the Tana village as soon as the court cases were over. Meanwhile the corporal in charge of the game scout post up river was to go there at once and take the thunder-flashes which George had sent back by Ibrahim. These were to frighten off the lions until he got there himself. George also sent instructions that no lions were to be shot before his arrival.

I passed on these instructions to the corporal, and he set off with the thunder-flashes, but, stopping on his way to buy tobacco, he heard that the local chief at the Tana had not only told his people to kill the lions but had also sent more game scouts of the neighbouring district to deal with the situation. The corporal instead of then making his way as rapidly as possible to the Tana to convey George's orders and to keep away the lions with his thunder-flashes, returned to camp to give me the account he had just heard. I was horrified at the loss of time, and sent him packing off to the Tana, praying that he might arrive before one or more of the cubs had been killed—if, indeed, the raiders were Elsa's children.

This happened on the 24th of March.

While all this was taking place I was stuck in camp, feeling ill and worried at not being able to walk about looking for spoor or even to move at all. Heavy rain pounded the river, across which I heard during the night the roars of several lions.

George arrived in the evening, and soon afterwards we heard a lion calling close to the camp; at dawn it moved towards the Hyrax Rock. George went out to investigate and found spoor belonging to a lioness; after leaving the neighbourhood of the camp she had apparently gone down river.

When he returned from this search, George set off in his Land-Rover for the scene of the last Tana raid. It had been raining heavily, so he was obliged to take a circuitous route. I remained in camp to keep a lookout in case the cubs were still in our area.

On the following day, as it was getting dark, I heard a lion roaring from the Big Rock; it was answered from farther away by another lion. Next I heard the roars advancing towards the kitchen lugga. Hoping that our cubs might be in the company of this lion, I told the men to prepare a meal for them. While this was being done, I was startled by a chorus of roars. It sounded as if there were lions on every side of the camp. Hurriedly we secured the meat inside my truck, and I advised the men to barricade themselves as best they could inside their thorn enclosure; I did the same myself and went to bed. There was no question of going to sleep for during the entire night we were kept awake by growls and whuffings which only at dawn ebbed away in the direction of the Big Rock.

In the morning I went to Elsa's grave, and while I was there noticed some movement on the Big Rock. Looking through my field-glasses, I saw two lions basking on top of the rock. I walked towards them as fast as my injured leg allowed, and soon distinguished three adult lions and three cubs exactly the size of Elsa's children. They were on top of the ridge, outlined against the sky. I watched them for several minutes; they were resting quietly together, one lioness licking the cubs who were rolling on their backs and playing. I took some photographs, but fearing that the distance was too great to get good results, even with my telescopic lens, I cautiously advanced towards the pride. When I was within about four hundred yards of them, the lions became alarmed and one after the other disappeared into the gap where Elsa had started her labour. Only one cub remained behind. It crouched with its head on its forepaws, watching me. This behaviour made me think that it was probably Jespah. Unfortunately, as it sat right against the morning sun, I could only see its silhouette and could not pick out any details to confirm its identity with Jespah. When I tried to come nearer, the cub sneaked away.

The idyllic family scene I had witnessed made me feel happier than I had felt since Elsa's death. Though I could not be quite sure that these were her children with their foster-parents, it seemed too great a coincidence that a pair of lions with three cubs exactly the same age as hers should suddenly have appeared near the camp.

After telling the men my exciting news, we put a carcase into the Land-Rover and I drove with Ibrahim near to the Big Rock, and placed the meat where I thought the lions would find it easily. Then we camouflaged the car with branches and waited inside to see what would happen. I hoped to take some more photographs when the cubs reappeared, and so be able to identify them.

We waited till 11 o'clock; by then the sun was getting hot,

the wind changed and was blowing in the wrong direction, and to my disappointment, no vultures had appeared to guide the lions to the kill. I therefore decided to move the carcase near the Whuffing Rock, but before doing this I went back to camp to leave a message for George in case he should return and want to join us. He had now been away two nights and I expected him back during the day.

When I reached the tents I was greeted by two game scouts with a letter from George. This is what he wrote:

'Got to the settlement on the evening of Sunday 26th, after travelling forty miles over bad roads and eight through thick bush. Managed to get a carcase and sat over it close to a Boma which the lions had raided. No lions came that night. In the morning I made camp some two miles from the village on the banks of the Tana and walked down the river to look for spoor. Saw nothing fresh. Later the scouts arrived to report that the lions had tried to enter another Boma during the night but were driven off. The scouts had followed their spoor but lost it. Yesterday evening I again sat up over a carcase in a clearing half a mile from this other Boma. About 11 p.m. without any warning, Little Elsa suddenly appeared and pounced on the carcase which was fastened to a tree stump. She was followed immediately by Jespah, who had an arrow, fortunately not poisoned, sticking in his rump. Both started to eat. Presently I saw Gopa lurking in the distance. Finally he also came to the meat. They were extremely thin and looked starved. They showed no fear when I talked to them and finished off the diminutive goat in an hour. They frequently came up of their own accord to the bowl of water I had placed close to the back of the car. I am confident that they recognised my voice and I am sure that they will come again to-night. There is no doubt that it is the cubs that have been raiding the Bomas. We will have to pay lots of compensation. Send Ibrahim with your Land-Rover at once with all the goats, some more food for me, also my small tent, table, chair and my boxes. I must immediately take on a gang of local men to cut a track, and then we will have to move the whole camp and get a lorry here with crates and finally move the cubs out of this district. But the most urgent thing is to send the goats with Ibrahim. If the river is too high, he will have to go the long way round, but he *must* get here to-day. The cubs are very hungry and will certainly raid another Boma unless I feed them. There is no doubt that all the trouble has been caused by the Fierce Lioness who must have chased the cubs away from Elsa's camp on 4th March.

Yours, G. Please send all my ammunition.

Chapter Nine

CRISIS

When I read this I felt as if all my blood were draining away from me. At first I could not get over my surprise at the extraordinary coincidence that a pride with three cubs of the same size as Elsa's should arrive in the area just now and thus deceive us into thinking that Jespah, Gopa and Little Elsa were still around the camp.

Then I remembered the pride to which Elsa, when she herself was pregnant, had given her goat and acted as aunt. Was it possible that the Fierce Lioness was the mother of these cubs, born perhaps just before Elsa's? If so, it seemed likely that the area around the camp had been the territory of this lioness before Elsa's release there. In this case, when the Fierce Lioness discovered a rival—and one that kept strange company with human beings—she might have withdrawn up river and brought up her cubs there. I remembered the day last July, when we were looking for Elsa and thought we saw the family near a baobab tree upstream and were astonished at their strange behaviour. Now I wondered whether we might not have mistaken this lioness, whom we have come to call the Fierce Lioness, and her cubs for Elsa's family. When, later, she had reconnoitred the camp, she had always come from up river. She had come alone, but she might well have preferred to leave her cubs in safety when she was on a scouting expedition. If this supposition were true, then the Fierce Lioness's attacks on Elsa were no doubt an attempt to re-establish her right to her old home. On these occasions she had found us in residence as well, and had retreated. But now that Elsa was dead what could be more probable than that she had jumped at the opportunity to chase her rival's cubs away and take possession of her old territory? However this might be, it seemed almost certain that the pride, this morning, I had taken to be Elsa's cubs was the family of the Fierce Lioness.

This was an anticlimax to the happiness I had felt a few hours earlier, when I believed the cubs were safe and well and exonerated from raiding the Tana bomas.

How they had managed to survive on their own for several weeks, I could not imagine. They were too young to know how to hunt wild animals successfully and they must have gone through a ghastly period of starvation before they came upon the goats which they would regard as their natural food. The angry reception from the enraged tribesmen must have terrified them. On the other hand, the tribesmen could not be blamed for defending their stock. The only hope now was to pay such heavy compensation that they would not be in too great a hurry to get rid of the cubs, and at the same time to find a safe place for the family with the least possible delay.

Since there was no longer anything to keep me in camp, I set off with Ibrahim, with a scout as a guide, five goats and all our essential camping material. We were very cramped, and the second scout and the rest of our staff had to take the short cut through the bush on foot.

We jolted along over very rough tracks; the country around looked as though some giant had amused himself by throwing rocks about at random. Now and then we passed small African settlements nestling among enormous boulders; the round earth huts resembled mounds and blended perfectly into the landscape.

We reached the Tana just before dark. The river here was about four hundred yards wide; tall trees grew along the banks and a narrow belt of undergrowth provided the only touch of colour. The flat hinterland covered with dense bush was dry, grey and dusty. We had dropped in altitude and it was much hotter here than in Elsa's camp.

From this point the scout had to guide us on foot over the last eight miles, for the bush was so thick that it was impossible to see any distance ahead or to avoid obstacles. The poor man got mercilessly scratched by thorns, and I gave him credit for the way in which, reconnoitring in the dark by the light of a small torch (our headlamps only blinded him), he found a way for the car to advance slowly, dodging trees and anti-bear holes, laying bushes flat and crossing deeply eroded river beds, some of which were flooded.

After two long hours of crashing through the bush, we found ourselves on the bank of a fast flowing river some hundred and fifty feet wide. We took the fanbelt off and plunged down a steep bank, and after a lot of pushing knee-deep in water, reached the other side.

Here we found the boma of the headman, but we went on another two miles to George's camp. There we were told that he was sitting up for the cubs. I dropped all my kit and drove on to join him, arriving at about 9 p.m. George, usually sparing of compliments, greeted me approvingly with : ' How the devil did you manage to get through this bush in the dark?'

While we waited for the arrival of the cubs, intermittently switching on a powerful spotlight to guide them, George told me about Jespah's wound.

On the night of the 25th a number of tribesmen set out to kill the lions. They cornered one of them (in fact Jespah) in the thorn enclosure which protected a flock of goats. The lion had killed two of the goats but before it could get away with its spoils was surrounded by a band of angry tribesmen, armed with bows and poisoned arrows. The lion took cover in the thick thorn fence, and into this the Africans shot about twenty arrows. Luckily the fence was so thick that the arrows did not penetrate. Only one shot loosed by a toto found its mark. Fortunately the arrowhead was not lethal, as the toto was too young to be trusted by his elders with the deadly poison.

The arrowhead had luckily not penetrated deeply into Jespah's rump. The barb and three inches of the shaft could clearly be seen running under the skin, one inch of the shaft hung downwards. George hoped that its own weight might cause the head to fall out and, as Jespah could easily lick the wound, there was a good chance of his keeping it free from infection. It did not seem to hinder his movements, nor could it be causing him any pain, since George had often seen him lie on it. The cubs were very friendly and did not object to his presence, but of course there was no question of Jespah allowing him to remove the arrowhead.

George had engaged thirty Africans to cut an eight-mile track along the river; this would enable us to bring up our whole camp in the lorry. He had also taken on four trackers to help with spooring, and had promised very generous compensation to the owners of raided stock. He told me that far from showing any hostility the tribesmen seemed very glad to get the compensation and the chance of earning good wages, which provided unknown luxuries.

George suggested that it might be better if I spent the night in camp in case the cubs should turn up there; so after calling ' cu-cu-coo ' and their names for a long time but getting no response, I drove back. As we were all too exhausted to pitch a tent, we quickly put up my camp bed and I slept in the open, hoping that it would not rain.

Next morning I was woken by the plop of a doam-palm nut which fell close to me. I took this as a good omen, for if it had fallen on my head it could easily have killed me. George came back for breakfast; he had seen no sign of the cubs, nor had the game scouts who had been guarding the huts with their thunder-flashes. George then went off spooring with Nuru; he was the only African the cubs knew and his presence was unlikely to make them bolt.

Our camp site was right on the Tana at a watering place, and hardly had George left than we were invaded by an enormous herd of goats and cattle. In a few minutes we were wrapped in a thick blanket of dust through which bleating and mooing animals stampeded to drink. Since we were certain to have daily visitations of this kind, the only thing to do was to move camp. I strolled along the river to look for a better site, keeping in the shade of the trees along the bank, for the heat was intolerable. Here the Tana flowed in a wide curve; there were many rapids and a number of small islands covered with rich vegetation. On some sandbanks I saw crocodiles basking in the sun. Between the large palm-trees and dense undergrowth which bordered the river there were a number of narrow paths evidently made by hippo.

Finally I found a good camping site. The approach to the river was not too steep, so that the boys would be able to get water for use in camp. By clearing the thick undergrowth we could make enough level space to pitch our few tents. The bank here was some ten feet above the river and formed a kind of barrier between the water and the lower-lying hinterland, which was like a simmering furnace compared with the comfortable shade of the vegetation along the bank.

George returned about two o'clock from a fruitless search. His face was almost purple and he was dripping with perspiration. I felt sorry for him. Luckily, the river near our bank was shallow enough for him to plunge in and cool off without running the risk of being nibbled by a croc.

After he had had his bath, he told me how during the morning he had saved the life of a water buck. Nuru had drawn his attention to a black object in the middle of the river some three hundred yards downstream. Looking through his field-glasses, George saw that it was a water buck, and simultaneously noticed five Wakamba poachers on the bank urging their dogs to go into the water after it. He thought the poachers must have seen him, so he fired a shot into a tree above their heads to warn them off. But apparently they had not noticed him and, taken by surprise, began to run in his direction. George and Nuru tried to cut them off but, being outnumbered, did not succeed. The poachers disappeared into the thick bush, all but one who swam across the river.

Later we moved the camp, taking care to avoid the hippo paths.

We then made plans for solving our immediate problem. George decided to sit up at night inside his Land-Rover on routes which he thought the cubs would take to reach the bomas; he would have meat placed ready for them. I would do the same at the camp, while the scouts, equipped with thunder-flashes, would protect the various bomas. Should any of us see the cubs we would warn George by firing shots : one if the scouts sighted them, two if I did.

When it got dark, George left for his vigil, but on this night the cubs took a different route, raided a boma and mauled a sheep; before they were able to feed they were driven off by the scouts' thunder-flashes.

It rained during the night, which made tracking difficult next day. Hoping to guide the cubs to his Land-Rover, George dragged a carcase through the bush to it, thinking they might pick up the scent; but next morning it turned out that only hyenas and jackals had come for the meal. Consequently, next night the cubs tried their luck at yet another boma and mauled two goats; again before being able to eat they were chased off.

The rains were due to start very soon and we were worried because, when this happened, we would be immobilised if we did not have a four-wheel-drive lorry. The old Thames lorry was useless in virgin bush and we could not borrow Ken Smith's Bedford truck for an indefinite time. We also needed a lorry to bring up our camp kit, to help the labour gang and, above all, for the final move when we had caught the cubs. Indeed, for this we should need two lorries; for we saw the convoy as comprising a lorry for the lions, a lorry for our camp kit, and two Land-Rovers to carry our personal luggage. It was essential that these cars should not be overloaded in case they were required to tow the lorries through bad patches.

Having talked this over, I decided that I had better go to Isiolo and order a new Bedford lorry, the same size as Ken's, on which the three travelling crates, already ordered, could be loaded.

Next morning, after hearing that the cubs had tried to raid two bomas but had been driven off before doing any damage, I started off with our faithful Ibrahim.

When I inquired about ordering a new Bedford lorry, I was told that delivery would take about three weeks. This was very inconvenient, so I asked if in case of an emergency we could hire a truck from a safari firm. This I was told was possible, and after making the necessary arrangements I started back in Ken's truck to Elsa's camp to pick up the kit we had left behind and to sleep there.

The aloes we had planted around Elsa's grave were now in

bloom; I was very surprised to see that their flowers were a whitish green, for the usual colour is salmon and it was by chance that we had transplanted this rare species from Isiolo. A very curious plant which I had never seen was growing at the base of the cairn. It had no stalk, was of an orange colour, cup-shaped and looked waxy; at its centre there was a sticky substance which exuded a smell like musk and from the rim of the cup a number of petals converged, like tentacles, inwards. It reminded me of the insect-eating parasite, Hydnora. I took some photographs of it and, later, identified it as Thonningia Balanophoraceae which was only known to grow on the west coast of Africa.

The night was very still and the soft moonlight blended everything into a peaceful harmony. I lay awake and late in the night heard the cubs' father circling the camp, whuffing, and afterwards moving to the Big Rock, finally crossing the river. I saw the Southern Cross, first over Elsa's grave, and watched it until dawn when it pointed towards the Tana. This was the last night I spent in our old camp which had been like a home to me.

While the men were breaking camp I went to the studio lugga and walked down river passing places which held most poignant memories for me. I heard baboons barking on the Whuffing Rock which made my anguish still more acute, as they had so often heralded the arrival of Elsa and her family. I tried to interpret their bush-telegraph as if they would urge me to hurry back to the Tana and help the cubs.

We arrived about tea-time, and George greeted me with the news that although he had tracked every day and sat up every night he had not once seen the cubs, but each night they had raided a boma. He was very worried, because in spite of their recent forays, they had, so far as he knew, not eaten for ten days, since they had always been driven away from the bomas before they could eat their kill. Unless they had killed a dikdik in the bush they must be ravenously hungry, and he feared that sooner or later they would injure someone. Their hunting ranged over eight miles of dense bush country. The fact that they never attacked the same boma on two successive

nights made it impossible for George to anticipate their moves.
Twice Jespah had even got into a hut. On the first occasion
a woman asleep inside with her goats round her was woken by
a bleat from her pet billygoat and saw Jespah's jaws clamp
round its throat. She shrieked, and Jespah dropped the goat
and tried to make his escape. In the mêlée the hut collapsed;
fortunately no one was injured. Undaunted, Jespah on the
following night entered a hut occupied by a youth, also surrounded by goats. The boy woke up to find Jespah's rump
protruding from under his bed as he tried to rake out a goat
which had taken shelter there. The boy yelled and kicked, and
Jespah decamped.

George looked worn out with sleepless nights, anxiety and
the worry of knowing that his work was piling up at Isiolo,
but while the present crisis lasted he could not leave the Tana
for a single night.

During my absence he had conceived a new plan. He
wanted to cut a straight track, fourteen miles long, from where
we were to Elsa's camp, and had already engaged a labour
gang to work on it. Luckily there was a much-frequented
elephant path which followed part of the route and would reduce the work required. The new truck would make it possible
for us to have a mobile camp and follow the movements of the
cubs; George also hoped that, by laying meat along it, each
night a little farther from the bomas, we should be able to
start trying to trap the cubs as soon as we had reached a safe
distance.

He thought that we might as well begin at once to guide the
cubs in this direction, so that afternoon he dragged a carcase
through the bush and lit a big fire. The cubs did not appear.
Instead, they tried to raid a boma half a mile away. Next
morning a tracker reported the spoor of a single lion heading
in the direction of Elsa's camp, but he had lost the pug marks
eventually by the river opposite the scout post.

That evening about 9 p.m. as George was sitting up over
the meat, he suddenly saw Jespah and Little Elsa. They were
terribly emaciated and the arrow was still in Jespah's rump.
Neither, however, seemed nervous, and Jespah licked the

cod-liver oil out of the pie-dish which George held out to him. They ate ravenously and did not leave till 5 a.m. After this, we thought it likely that Gopa had deserted his brother and sister and that it was his spoor the tracker had seen heading in the direction of the old camp. We therefore sent a runner with instructions to the scouts who were keeping an eye on Elsa's camp to feed Gopa if he turned up, and to let us know if he did.

George spent the rest of the day paying out heavy compensation to the tribesmen; in the evening he waited at a place close to where he thought the cubs were lying-up. It rained all night; the cubs did not appear. Instead, they had gone to the spot where they had seen him the night before, and not finding him there had raided three bomas, killed two goats and mauled six others. In the morning the trackers who were following the spoor caught sight of two bolting cubs.

Later a scout arrived from Elsa's camp and reported that during the night of the 5th/6th April a young lion had been there and had left his pug marks all over the place where George usually pitched his tent; afterwards he had gone off towards the Big Rock. On the following night he had returned in the company of a big lion. The latter did not come into camp but crossed the river. The young lion had gone first to the tree we used as a 'bush-fridge,' then to Elsa's grave, and finally into the old crate. This confirmed our belief that it must be Gopa. No doubt disgusted at being chased out of the bomas before he could get a meal, hunger had prevailed over his natural timidity and he had made the journey home on his own, hoping to find us in camp with a square meal ready for him.

Since the two scouts who were over at the camp were unfamiliar with the cubs' habits we sent Nuru back to feed Gopa. As soon as it was possible to cross the flooded river by car, I intended to join him. If Gopa were to act as a guide to the other cubs and induce them to return to Elsa's camp, this would greatly facilitate our task. But unless and until this happened our problem would be even greater than before Gopa's departure. It had been difficult enough to follow the cub's movements, and try to prevent them from carrying out their raids when they were all together, but trying to control two danger areas fourteen miles apart, at a time when rain made movement by car nearly impossible, was a nightmare.

That night the cubs passed within a hundred yards of George on their way from a boma where they had eaten part of a dead goat which the tribesmen had thrown out. We were desperate. All we could do was to reinforce the thorn enclosures around all the bomas and set scouts to guard as many of them as possible; but there were not enough scouts to go round.

As the back axle of George's Land-Rover had broken, he had sent Ibrahim by car to Isiolo to get a new one. Meanwhile, George was obliged to spend his nights in a small tent. That evening, after he had gone to his night's vigil, I went for a stroll. All day the sky had been clouding up and the atmosphere was oppressive and heavy with rain. Suddenly I heard some deep, sonorous grunts and saw two hippo in the middle of the river blowing jets of water into the air each time they surfaced. The sinking sun turned from bright orange, then to a very deep red and finally to purple. Silhouetted against this ball of fire was a group of doam-palm trees, their fronds delicately outlined against the dramatic background until the light faded, all forms were lost, and everything had blended into a grey sea of bush. Then I became aware of an exquisite scent and followed it up until I came upon a Sesamothamnus Busseanus Engl bush. This small tree, which usually grows in waterless country, cannot afford to put out leaves and flowers at the same time. Now it was in blossom and its large white velvety blooms were all the more striking because they grew on bare, thorny branches. The strongly-scented buds open only after sunset, offering their nectar to nocturnal insects. One night was all their life. When the first rays of the rising sun streaked the sky, they fell to the ground. So much splendour for one night only—and remembering the blood-red sunset clouds pregnant with rain, I wondered whether these particular flowers would be granted even that short span.

My thoughts were interrupted by the noise of a car, and I knew that Ibrahim had returned. He told me that the river was rising rapidly owing to the heavy rain up-country; in fact he had only just managed to get across.

Soon after I went to bed it started to pour. I felt worried about George, sitting up in this deluge in his small tent surrounded by lions; also the hippos' booming sounded very much closer to my tent than I cared for. But in spite of these anxieties, I dozed off.

I woke suddenly, conscious of a rhythmic swish-swishing noise, but as it was mixed up with the drumming of the rain on the canvas of my tent and the roaring of the flooded Tana a few feet away, I could not make out what it was—perhaps a broken branch brushing against my tent. I paid no attention to it. Then one of my tent-poles collapsed. I flashed my torch and saw that the swishing was made by waves lapping against my tent.

We had pitched camp about nine feet above the normal water level; within three hours the water of the Tana had risen by this amount. In whatever direction I looked I could see nothing but water. By the beam of my torch I could see that the hinterland was already a swamp pocked with deep pools, and this was the only place to which we could move—if the river did not get there first; another foot rise, and the water would sweep over it.

I was near to panic. I yelled to the boys, but their tents were about two hundred yards away, and in the thundering roar of of the Tana they could not hear me. I ran over to them as fast as I could. The flaps of their tents were tightly fastened and they were all sound asleep in what were now proper traps. Indeed, if I had not reached them when I did, they might all have been drowned.

As soon as they staggered out, they realised the danger. First they pulled down George's large tent, which held our rifles, medicines, food and kit. It was already half-flooded, so we dumped all we could snatch in the hinterland and then pulled down my smaller tent. My torch was the only one which worked, but soon this too dropped into the water and was useless. I thought how lucky it was that Ibrahim had returned with the axle, for he organised the panic-stricken men and got most of our kit out of the torrent.

We were safe for the time being, but I realised that unless a miracle happened it would only be a matter of minutes before the hinterland, our only refuge, was also flooded.

I stuck a stick into the mud to mark the water level, and watched it anxiously. I could hardly believe my eyes when I saw that the water remained at the same level; the flood had reached its full height just before it would have carried our camp away.

Quickly, we set about rescuing George's Land-Rover, which was immobile without its back axle and half covered by the flood. Luckily it was close to a tree and, with an improvised pulley, we were able to hoist it and keep it suspended above the water, so that it could not be swept away. Again, I was glad that Ibrahim was there to help with the operation. When it was completed we waited, drenched and exhausted, for dawn to break.

At first light George arrived, stiff, cold and wet. He told us that before the rain started Jespah and Little Elsa had arrived and eaten an enormous meal and left soon afterwards. When the downpour began all the tent-poles gave way and the tent collapsed on top of George. For the rest of the night he had huddled beneath the wet canvas. He felt very uneasy, for if the cubs had returned to investigate the wreckage he would have been quite helpless. But Little Elsa and Jespah were, as it later proved, otherwise occupied, for in spite of having eaten so heartily they had gone off to a boma and killed a goat.

By breakfast-time the river had fallen six feet. Scanning the lashing waves with field-glasses, I saw amongst the debris a dinghy perched upside down on the top of a tree growing on one of the islands. I also observed a beautiful Goliath heron on the opposite bank; he was smashing a fish in rapid strokes against a rock. I thought how hard he had to work to prepare his breakfast.

Chapter Ten

PREPARATIONS FOR TRAPPING
THE CUBS

SURVEYING OUR POSITION, we decided that the safest course was to pitch our tents in the bushy hinterland, close to some big trees, in whose shade we could spend the heat of the day.

I laid out our soaked belongings to dry in the sun, while George went in search of the cubs. He did not find them but that night, as he sat up in my car with a meal ready, Jespah and Little Elsa arrived, ate ravenously and stayed till 11 p.m. In the early hours of the morning George heard both cubs roaring. So far as he knew, this was their first attempt, and though the sound was a little immature, it was quite a creditable performance. We wondered whether they were calling to Gopa—or asserting their right to their new territory.

On the following night the two cubs came in early, ate half the meal George had prepared for them, and then, when it started to rain, went off and apparently out of sheer devilment attacked a boma, killing three goats and mauling four more.

Meanwhile, I had excitements of my own. I had pitched my tent near a large bush, from which I hoped to get a maximum of shade. I had not noticed that the spot I had chosen was right in the middle of a hippo path. During the night I heard the beast approach to within a few yards, then luckily it turned back and plunged into the river. As it was raining hard I knew that I could not move the tent till morning; by then everything had again collapsed and all our kit was standing in several inches of water. The boxes in which I kept my correspondence were awash and their contents reduced to a soggy pulp. I carefully extracted some important files and laid them out to dry, though already the writing had been reduced to a vague blur. We spent the whole day trying to dry out possessions, but sudden downpours defeated our efforts. It was a day of complete confusion; yet not without some compensation: as I was struggling with our belongings I suddenly saw a palm-leaf caught in one of the sun's rays. Its wet fronds glistened against the deep blue sky and it seemed to me that nothing could be more beautiful than the perfect design of that leaf.

That evening, on his way to the cubs, George got bogged down in the mud. When he arrived he found Jespah and Little Elsa waiting for him, and for some time he sat in the dark and heard them contentedly eating the meal he had provided. Later, when he switched on his headlights, he was surprised to see three cubs. Gopa must just have arrived, for he was formally greeting his brother and sister. When this ceremony was over, he got down to the meat and would not let the other cubs come near it. He must have been very hungry, but looked fit. He had been away for over a week, and George thought that during this time he must have had at least two good meals or he would not have been in such good condition. All the cubs took their cod-liver oil, after which they went off in the direction of the bomas. George fired a warning shot, so the scouts were on the alert when the cubs arrived and greeted them with thunder-flashes which scared them off.

Although, up to now, the cubs had not collaborated in our plans to catch them in the crates, we thought it essential that everything should be ready for their capture. Day by day the weather was getting worse, and it was vital that we should get the crates up before the rain made transport by lorry impossible.

The fourteen-mile track through the bush had now been cut. It was very rough even by comparison with the one we had used to get to the Tana, but at least it would greatly shorten the journey. Another advantage was that the river we had to cross on this route was fairly narrow where we intended to ford it. Though the approaches to it were steep, it was a much better alternative than the river on the old track, which was a hundred and fifty yards wide and probably impassable in flood.

To collect all the things we required, I set off with Ibrahim for Isiolo. We had great difficulty in crossing the river even at the narrow ford, and our troubles were not improved by the arrival of a drunken headman. However, we reached the other side and as we drove along the new track I made notes of many places where improvements were needed if we were to use this route with a lorry full of cubs.

While at Isiolo I heard from Major Grimwood that after negotiating with a number of game reserves he had obtained permission for us to take the cubs to the Serengeti National Parks in Tanganyika. I was most grateful to him and extremely pleased, for the Serengeti is famous for lions and an abundance of game; I felt that we could not have found a better home for Elsa's cubs.

I wrote to the Director of the National Parks, thanking him for his generous offer and pointing out that for a month or two at least the cubs would still need our help, since they were only sixteen months old; and at least a short time ago still had their milk teeth and would not be able to hunt independently until they were two years. Of course I also mentioned that Jespah had an arrow in his rump.

When I made inquiries about the lorry I had ordered I was told that it was still in the docks at Mombasa, so I hired a similar model from Ker-Downey Safari. We could not risk a delay in case we missed an opportunity to catch the cubs. Major Grimwood kindly agreed to allow us to keep Ken Smith's Bedford and use it for the move. Having got the truck problem settled, I speeded up the completion of the three box-traps, ordered pulleys, ropes, car-batteries, a further supply of Librium, photographic materials and drew a lot of money from the bank. I also got a doctor to look at my leg. During the last few weeks I had been dressing it under most un-hygienic conditions, but in spite of this treatment the wound was beginning to heal, though it was still deep and open.

It rained without stopping while I was at Isiolo and I itched to get back before we were cut off by the floods. When I finally arrived, complete with three crates and the Ker-Downey lorry, George told me that the cubs had come to him during each of the four nights I had been absent, and that though they had tried to make some raids they had been driven off before any damage was done. The precautions he had taken—reinforcing the thorn enclosures, guarding the most vulnerable homes with scouts and giving a warning shot when he suspected that the cubs were bent on mischief—had proved successful.

George described how on one occasion he had given the cubs two guinea-fowl. This had immediately started a fight; with guinea-fowl available they showed no interest in the carcase he had put out for them. He said that Little Elsa was limping badly, probably from a thorn in one of her pads, but as she was as wild as ever he could do nothing to help her.

The cubs were now in excellent condition. Jespah still carried the arrowhead in his rump, but it did not appear to cause him any discomfort or interfere with his movements. They had recovered their trust in George and were quite at ease as he walked amongst them while they fed, refilling their water bowl and their pie-dishes of cod-liver oil. Nor was it only during the hours of darkness that they proved trustful. The day before, in broad daylight, George had come upon them asleep under a bush. They had shown no alarm and only slowly moved a short distance before settling down to sleep again.

This was certainly an improvement, but we still felt as though we were living on a volcano. True, the cubs, even when desperately hungry and driven off their kills, had never attempted to injure anyone; true, the tribesmen had shown great patience and been very helpful—indeed, they seemed well pleased with their compensation and the ready market provided for their surplus goats—none the less it was worrying to reflect that the bush all round us was swarming with herds of goats and sheep and that these herds were in the charge of small children. The sooner the cubs were captured and removed the better for everybody.

To this end, we cleared an opening in the bush close to the place where they were in the habit of lying-up during the day. There we placed the three crates side by side. George suspended their trapdoors by ropes running through pulleys fastened to a straight tree-trunk which he had secured horizontally above the crates by driving both ends into the forks of the two trees between which the crates stood. Having done this, he brought the ends of the three ropes together and spliced them into a single rope; this he tied with a slip knot to a tree about twenty yards in front of the crates where he intended to wait inside his Land-Rover. Thus, if the three cubs entered separate crates, all he had to do was to release the rope and all three trapdoors would fall simultaneously.

The first thing to do was to accustom the cubs to feed in the crates, and then wait for the critical moment. For eleven nights now they had come more or less regularly to be fed by George, so to entice them from the vicinity of the bomas and in the direction of the traps, he gradually moved the place at which he fed them towards the crates. When he had lured the cubs to within a quarter of a mile of them he attached two carcases to the Land-Rover and when the cubs appeared slowly towed the meat towards the box-traps. Jespah promptly foiled his scheme by swinging a carcase round a tree-trunk causing the rope to break.

On the next night George had better luck, for the cubs followed their dinner right up to the crates. When they appeared the cubs did not show any fear of the large boxes— Gopa even sat inside one of them while he ate his meal.

At last it looked as though we might capture the cubs fairly soon. This was a great relief, but George now had another worry to do with his work—while he had been on the Tana coping with the cubs he had been obliged to neglect his ordinary duties. If he moved the cubs to the Serengeti, he would be absent for a long time, since we would hope to camp there until the cubs had settled down and no longer depended on us.

The Serengeti was seven hundred miles distant from Isiolo, so it would no longer be possible for him to divide his time between his work and the cubs, as he had done up to now. So far Major Grimwood had most loyally defended him against outside criticism, but George hated to exploit his senior's kindness. The only solution he could see was to resign from his job so that he could devote his time exclusively to the cubs. He therefore wrote a letter of resignation to Major Grimwood. I knew what this decision cost George, who for twenty-two years had devoted his life to his work. Indeed I had only to look at his strained face and see how thin he had grown to understand what these last weeks had meant to him.

I thought that it might be a help to him if I could find a professional trapper to assist him in capturing the cubs, and that I should go to Isiolo to try to contact one. We also wanted to remove the arrowhead from Jespah's rump. George had asked the elders who could still remember tribal warfare how they used to extract arrows embedded in flesh. They said that they twiddled the shaft and thus loosened the barb with less damage to the flesh than if it were pulled straight out. We didn't think that Jespah would allow us to do much twiddling, so George invented a device consisting of a larger copy of the barb, with razor-sharp edges. This he hoped to slip under the arrowhead and then pull both out together without enlarging the wound more than was necessary. To do this would involve confining Jespah in a crate and it could be done after the three cubs were trapped and before they started the journey to the Serengeti. So, to get the spray, find a trapper and get some chains for our four-wheel-drive vehicles, I set off for Isiolo with Ibrahim. We travelled in Ken's Bedford lorry which needed repairs and had some nasty moments when the huge five-ton truck skidded on the wet road. The sky was black and there was plainly more rain coming, so I was in a great hurry to get back before conditions got any worse.

Luckily it only took me one day to make all my purchases. As no professional trapper was available, I rang up Julian McKeand who had been with us and Elsa on the foot safari described in *Born Free*, and had since become a white hunter. He agreed to help and promised to join us next morning. I also rang up John Berger as well as another vet at Nairobi, both living along the route we should take with the cubs, and asked them if they would operate on Jespah if we passed at a convenient time, for I was doubtful whether the freezing spray would take effect on Jespah's thick pelt and didn't want to risk an operation that might be a failure.

Some time ago we had an inquiry from an American magazine asking whether we would help one of their reporters to photograph the capture of the cubs. Since at the time we could not foresee when the capture might take place, we left the matter open. I was therefore surprised to find three cables announcing the arrival of a photographer in the course of the next few days, and still more surprised when on the following morning he rang up from Nairobi saying that he had just arrived. Since he could not get to Isiolo until late on the following afternoon, I had to delay my return to George and the cubs for twenty-four hours. This worried me because of the likelihood that the rains would increase but as the man had travelled so far, and as his picture of the cubs might help to promote sympathy for game reservations, I decided to wait.

We had already launched the Elsa Appeal, donations to which go to help animals who live in areas where their presence clashes with the interests of human beings, with the result that they must either be removed or destroyed. As only limited funds are available for this purpose, many animals are doomed. We hoped with funds from the Elsa Appeal to subsidise rescue teams to save animals who were under a death sentence. The fact that since we had started the fund Elsa's children were themselves doomed, unless our improvised and experimental efforts succeeded, seemed to me a bitter irony. If an article appearing in a paper that had a vast circulation would help to win sympathy for the project of rescue teams, then I would have done well to postpone my journey.

When Julian arrived, I told him how we planned to capture the cubs. He strongly advised taking the large communal crate over to the camp. He thought it might be much easier to catch the cubs in this and afterwards move them into separate crates, for he doubted whether they would each simultaneously enter a separate crate. We could not of course risk trying to capture them separately, as the first to be caught would be certain to warn the others.

So we loaded the lorry with the cumbersome communal crate, filled with as many goats as it would hold; Julian took his Land-Rover so that he could move independently. It rained all day, and I gave the pilot who brought the photographer full marks for finding his way in this foul weather and landing safely on the slippery airfield.

Having lived for so many years in Kenya, I had learned that here one was far more dependent on weather conditions than in Europe; plans often fell literally into the water and disintegrated. I therefore listened with apprehension to the photographer who had been rushed from Berlin to Kenya, as he told me that he had allowed himself just three days to photograph the capture of the cubs at our distant and by now probably inaccessible camp before hurrying off to Cuba for his next assignment.

During the night the rain poured down as though it were coming through a hose. I wondered how we should ever make our way to the camp and felt sorry for the photographer who was likely to be in for a disagreeable experience. My fears were not unfounded, for all along the road cars were slithering about in and out of deep ruts, their drivers fighting to avoid landing in a ditch or colliding with other vehicles; sudden cloudbursts made the situation still worse. I travelled on the lorry with the men and the goats; the photographer and Julian travelled in the Land-Rover. Our progress was slow. Long before we reached the river, the roaring of its torrent told me that we were not going to be able to get across. Nearly nine feet of raging water was flowing between the steep banks. All we could do was to camp beside the river for the night and hope that by morning the level would have fallen. Luckily Julian had brought a double tent, which he shared with the photographer for whom I felt a great deal of sympathy, as the discomfort was considerable and he was not used to safari conditions. I myself used a small mountain tent I had brought along in case of an emergency like this.

Next morning we saw that the water instead of falling had risen to a still higher level. There was nothing to be done except send two scouts across country—a distance of not more than fifteen miles in a straight line through the bush—to tell George of our predicament and to ask him to send us his Land-Rover along the newly-cut track and, when the water receded, to tow us across. We then settled down to wait for our rescue party. Julian and the photographer sat in their tents discussing world affairs, and I sat in mine reading the mail I had collected in Isiolo but had not yet opened. In it I found a collection of newspaper cuttings with the most terrifying headlines:

'Elsa's cubs may have to be shot.'
'Death threats to Elsa's cubs.'
'Elsa's cubs: sentence of death.'

Chapter Eleven

THE CAPTURE

I WAS TERRIFIED. The reports stated that Major Grimwood had told reporters in Nairobi that he had instructed George to try to capture the cubs and transfer them to a game reserve, and that if he failed to do so he must shoot them. That Major Grimwood should tell the Press that he was giving such an order without first informing us was utterly unlike him. I felt sure then, as I afterwards discovered to be true, that the Press had misunderstood what he had told them. Certain as I was that Major Grimwood had not done this, I determined to conceal the cuttings from the photographer.

I knew, of course, that if the cubs scratched anyone, even slightly, they would be sentenced to death; mercifully they had not done so, but it was vital to move them as soon as possible, and meanwhile we had to remain inactive, facing the unfordable river. I tried to hide my anxiety but found it difficult to sympathise with the reporter's fears that he might not get back in time to catch his plane for Cuba, or to be polite about his complaint that I had not brought any coat-hangers for him.

Suddenly the rain stopped. Ibrahim and I anxiously watched the water slowly subsiding. As I feared that the scouts, making their way on foot to the camp, might have been delayed, I suggested that Julian should drive as near to the camp as he could, taking Ibrahim with him so that when they could go no farther in the Land-Rover Ibrahim could walk the rest of the way and deliver my message to George.

They set off, and after the car had reached its limit, Ibrahim plodded for many miles waist-deep through slush and, as I expected, reached the camp long before the scouts turned up. George was understandably surprised at the idea of receiving two guests under the present circumstances. He sent Ibrahim back to us in his Land-Rover, and at noon the next day we saw him waving cheerfully to us from the opposite bank.

The men carried our essential kit over the river, which was still far too deep for any vehicle to cross. Julian and the photographer tucked up their shorts and waded. I was carried across sitting on the clasped hands of two men : such a thing had never happened to me before, but as the wound in my leg was still open I dared not risk getting it infected in the chocolate-coloured water.

When we reached the far bank we squeezed into the Land-Rover. It was a tight fit with the three of us, our staff and our kit on board, but we managed it and were soon bumping along the newly-cut track.

Soon after our arrival, George took us to see the box-traps and demonstrated his device. We were all very much impressed when, as soon as he released the rope, the three doors crashed down simultaneously like guillotines, leaving a small gap to accommodate a protruding tail if necessary. No professional could have designed a better way of trapping the cubs, and I felt very proud of him.

He told us that the cubs had come every night and that each had entered a crate to eat the meat he had placed in it. Jespah had even spent a whole night inside one of them. The trouble was that sometimes two cubs would go into the same box; or if all three were in different crates, then a head or a rump would protrude beyond the door, making it impossible to use the guillotine device. Would they ever, all three, be at the same time in a position which would make it possible for us to capture them?

We arranged that the photographer should spend the night out with George, so that when the cubs appeared he could take pictures of them. He had not brought any flashlight apparatus with him, but was confident that his films were so fast that the lights of the car would provide sufficient illumination.

Soon after dark the cubs arrived. When they first heard the

voice of a stranger they bolted, but soon came back for their meal, and spent the whole night close to the car, apparently undisturbed by the clicking of the camera.

Next morning the photographer was in a great hurry to return, so after he had taken pictures of some camp scenes and some of the bomas which had suffered most severely from the cubs' attentions, he left our camp for Cuba.

Julian drove him back, intending to return with the new Bedford truck as soon as it was delivered. We hoped that his arrival might coincide with the capture of the cubs. When that happened he would be of great assistance to us, for we were very short-handed; all three drivers were down with malaria, two boys were suffering from dysentery and George was tired out. If Julian got back in time he would be able to supervise the breaking up of the camp and take charge of the rear, enabling us to move the cubs to their new home with the minimum delay.

We were full of hope that our anxieties might be nearing an end when the mail brought us a bombshell. George received a letter from the District Commissioner in whose area we now stayed, containing an ultimatum to capture the cubs within a stated period. The D.C. added that he was sorry to have to give this order, but since the situation was being exploited politically he could not give us his support after this date.

We were most distressed; for although we believed that we were nearing the time when we might hope to capture the cubs, we were working under great handicaps: my injured leg, sickness amongst our staff, the fact that since George's resignation could not take immediate effect he might be obliged to return to Isiolo, and the possibility that at any moment heavy rains might stop us. The one satisfactory thing was that for the last nine days the cubs had stopped raiding bomas and had come every night to George for their food.

It was the 24th April. I had not seen them since the 27th February, when Jespah had played with me on the Whuffing Rock. In the hope of seeing them again I joined George and after parking my car close to his, I prepared lumps of meat in which I concealed doses of terramycin and placed them inside the crates with the carcases. Then we waited inside our Land-Rovers.

Soon after dark I felt something brush against my car—it was Jespah. Silently he went straight to the crates, apparently unperturbed by finding a second car on the scene. He ate two of the titbits containing terramycin and then walked over to George, who was standing outside his car holding out a pie-dish of cod-liver oil. The cub licked it clean and then returned to his dinner. He showed no surprise at seeing me, and when I called ' Cucucoo' very softly, only cocked his ears for a moment and then went on with his meal. He had grown enormously and filled out, though he remained, like Elsa, a lion of slender build. The arrow was clearly visible under the skin of his rump, and the open wound was discharging a little, but it was not swollen and looked clean. From time to time he sat down and licked it. I was glad that it did not seem to hinder his movements.

Suddenly I heard a rustling in a bush behind my car and, flashing my torch, caught a glimpse of Gopa, some twenty yards away. For a quarter of an hour he remained there in hiding, then he was joined by Little Elsa. I called ' Cucucoo' to them, but so far from encouraging them, this caused Gopa to bolt twice, but in the end he could not resist the smell of the meat and cautiously sneaked up to the crates. He ate the lumps of meat and cleared out both pie-dishes of cod-liver oil before he started on the carcase. Little Elsa was extremely shy, and it was long after midnight before she ventured to approach the crates. By then all the terramycin and the cod-liver oil had been eaten by her brothers.

All the cubs were in good condition. Having seen the photographs George had taken of them when he had first found them on the Tana, which showed them as pathetic skeletons, I realised what an incredible job he had done. That they were now in splendid health and that their trust in us had been restored was entirely due to his patience and ingenuity. We watched them eating until 4 a.m. when they departed with heavy bellies.

Next morning we were obliged to send Ibrahim to Isiolo with urgent mail; the weather looked forbidding and we could only hope that he would not be too long delayed by his four-hundred-mile journey over slippery tracks.

That evening the cubs did not appear. We tried not to worry by reminding ourselves that after last night's dinner they did not need one this evening. During the night I heard a lion roar. We could not go out spooring next morning because heavy rain had washed away all pug marks. I was relieved when Jespah arrived at dark; but he paid us only a fleeting visit and about an hour later I heard him calling from far away. Meanwhile Gopa had put in a short appearance and hearing the call—trotted off. Eventually all three cubs arrived. Soon afterwards a lion roared, but they paid no attention to him. Jespah and Little Elsa were inside separate crates, busy with their dinner. Gopa visited them in turn, but finding himself unwelcome, sat down sulkily at the entrance to the third crate. Would he enter it? Should we be able to release the trapdoors and capture the cubs? The suspense was nerve-racking and increased by our fear that the lion we had recently heard might in time induce the cubs to follow him. If they did we should be unable to protect them from the death warrant or from the tribesmen's arrows.

The following night we again had cause to worry for at the first roar the cubs stopped eating, listened intently, dropped the meat and rushed off in the direction from which the calls came. They all returned later to finish their meal; but we could not help wondering whether they would always come back.

Ibrahim returned with the news that the new Bedford would not be ready for ten days. This was inconvenient, and it also meant that Julian would not come back to help us, for his plans did not permit of such a long delay. Another new worry was that whenever heavy rains fell—and they fell frequently—the roads were now to be officially closed to traffic.

Meanwhile our trackers had come in and reported that the cubs' spoor led in the direction of the wild lion. If we waited for the weather to improve and for the Bedford to arrive when the roads were reopened, the cubs might well by then have wandered off with the local lion and run into disaster.

That night they did not appear. I could imagine them having fun with their new friend, but I could also visualise the period of their reprieve running out. The one good factor was that in our area it had not rained for two days. The official closing of the roads operated on the basis of local conditions so that, if the rain held off and if the cubs *did* enter the crates, the weather at least would not prevent us from moving them from this area.

We spent the day improving the trapping device, rehearsing our parts in the capture and sharpening the scalpel with which George hoped to extract the arrowhead. In spite of these occupations the hours seemed to drag until it was time to sit up for the cubs.

I had barely finished the terramycin into the meat lumps when Jespah appeared. He ate two of them and then came and sat in front of our cars and watched us. Meanwhile his brother and sister entered separate crates. A little later they came out and lay near Jespah. They looked very lovely in the bright moonlight and I longed to remove them from the dangers which were increasing. But as if to mock me, the lion chose this moment to roar, and the cubs went off like a flash. I heard a hearty curse from George's car; another of the few remaining nights was lost. Resigned, I went to lie on my bed, asking George to call me when it was my turn to keep watch, or before that, if anything should happen. I felt very depressed but was so tired that I dozed off.

Suddenly I was woken by the crashing of the crate doors. A deathly silence followed; it was as if all life had suddenly stopped. After a short time the struggle inside the crates began. Simultaneously George and I ran to them, quickly removed the wooden blocks we had placed below the doors to prevent any damage to protruding tails, and closed the narrow slits so as to remove any opportunity for leverage and make an attempt to escape impossible.

Although it was in immense relief to know that the cubs were now safe, both George and I felt disgusted at the deception we had practised on them. Very grateful for the way in which George, single-handed, had effected the difficult capture, I kissed him, but he only gave a sad smile.

Chapter Twelve

THE JOURNEY TO THE SERENGETI

Now there was no time to lose if we wished to reduce the cubs' time of discomfort and bewilderment to a minimum. George remained on guard and I went back to camp, woke the men, told them the news, then, together, we hurriedly packed up, so as to be ready to hoist the cubs on to the truck at first light.

Dawn crept across the still moonlit sky and a new day began which was to mark a great change in all our lives.

When all was ready we drove the five-ton Bedford to the crates. George told me that after Jespah had recovered from the shock of finding himself trapped, he had calmed down and spent most of the night sitting quietly in his box. Little Elsa had followed his example, but Gopa had gone on fighting for a long time. Now he was growling savagely at our boys, who had come to help in hoisting the crates on to the truck.

Although we had told the tribesmen not to come near the lions, a chattering crowd soon collected. This terrified Gopa, who in his struggle broke one of the ceiling planks of his cage and split two others. We immediately covered the gap with a ground sheet, fixed iron bars across it and tied them on with thick ropes. Then we hoisted the crates, each of which weighed well over 800 lb. During this operation the Africans to induce the necessary impetus shouted in rhythm, which terrified the excited cubs. As the heavy boxes, lifted by block and tackle dangled in the air, the horrified lions paced to and fro, causing the crates to sway alarmingly. We hoisted Little Elsa first; her crate placed lengthwise to the side of the truck filled half its breadth. Gopa we placed alongside her, and his crate filled the other half. Both their wooden doors faced the back of the driver's cab. Jespah's crate we placed broadside across the end of the lorry. In this way the cubs had the fullest view of each other; only separated by the bars of the cages. It also had the advantage of making it possible to get at Jespah from the rear of the truck, so that we could try to extract his arrowhead as soon as an opportunity arose. For the moment there was no question of operating on him, as he was far too excited, but we hoped that later on either we or a vet might be able to remove it.

In their present state the cubs would not touch any food, so there was no chance of giving them tranquillisers. Luckily we knew that they had all had a good meal, and we had secured meat in each crate, as well as a water container which we refilled before covering the lorry with a ground sheet to protect the cubs from any low branches which might hit the truck during the journey.

We were ready to move; I took a last look to make sure that everything was in order: Jespah's expression was almost unendurable. Leaving the jabbering crowd behind, we proceeded in convoy: first my Land-Rover, followed by the lion lorry, then the Ker-Downey Bedford carrying our camping kit and some goats and the communal crate; George in his Land-Rover brought up the rear.

The first fourteen miles were very rough, the trucks bumping over boulders as they wound their way through dense shrub along the newly-cut track. In spite of the shaking, the cubs lay down and took the drive well.

We found the river still in flood, but just fordable. My Land-Rover and the lion lorry crossed safely, but messed up the banks so badly that the other cars couldn't make the gradient and had to be towed by the lion truck. This involved several reversings, occompanied by a lot of shouting which the lions endured resignedly.

Heavy rain clouds were gathering on every side; we were surrounded by a threatening black wall. Skidding through mud, we raced this colossal storm for sixty miles and won only by a hair's breadth. At dusk we reached the District H.Q., left a message for the District Commissioner telling him our good news, and then pressed on.

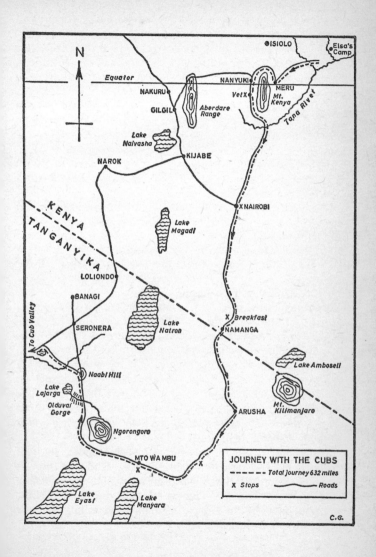

When we passed the boundary of the district I took a very deep breath: the cubs were now outside the jurisdiction of the death sentence. Looking back at the deluge which was following close behind us, I realised how narrowly we had escaped being imprisoned by floods.

Altogether we had more than seven hundred miles to travel. From now on most of the way lay through highlands which rose to 7,500 feet. We had started at an elevation of twelve hundred feet, and had now reached an altitude of seven thousand feet. Although we were actually crossing the Equator, it was bitterly cold. Above us, Mount Kenya's ragged, ice-covered peaks rose to seventeen thousand feet; they were covered with heavy cloud and drizzling rain fell upon us as we went along its base.

Up to now our little convoy had kept close together, and if one vehicle lagged behind we waited for it. At this point we lost sight of the Ker-Downey truck. George decided to go back and look for it; meanwhile the lion lorry and I were to go on to a little township where there was the vet who might be able to operate on Jespah. This was eighty miles ahead and it was nine in the evening before we reached it.

Even though the hour was so late, John Berger very kindly offered to try to extract the arrowhead there and then; but he was unable to do so because Jespah, when he saw the stranger, got into a rage and would not allow him to come near enough to administer the anæsthetic. The vet comforted me by saying that he thought if we waited for two or three weeks the arrow might well slough out by itself. In any case, the wound was only skin-deep, looked perfectly healthy and was not interfering with any vital function. In case the arrow did not come out of itself, he lent me some extra long bullet forceps, gave me some antiseptic, and suggested that we might be able to pull it out later on, if Jespah allowed us to perform the operation. By now George had joined us and we gratefully accepted the vet's offer of coffee, as we had had nothing to eat or drink since breakfast.

Warmed up, we pushed on. The weather got worse, the drizzling rain turned to a real downpour and it became icy cold. We stopped often to fasten the flapping tarpaulins to the cubs' lorry, and I felt very sorry for them when I saw them crouching in the farthest corners trying to avoid the drenching rain. All through the night we were at an altitude of five thousand feet, and I feared they might develop pneumonia. Twice we were held up by Askaris (African police) who were searching for a criminal, and it took us some time to convince them that there was no one concealed in our lorries—only three lions who had never harmed a human being.

We reached Nairobi at 3 a.m. and filled up the tanks. When the sleepy staff at the petrol station saw our lions they seemed to think they must be dreaming, and I didn't like to imagine what our passage through towns during daylight was going to be like.

The hours between 3 a.m. and daylight were a great strain on all of us. As we crossed the Kajiado Plain there were gusts of icy wind and several cloudbursts. Our drivers were worn out by their efforts to keep their vehicles on the slippery road. I took over from George, who couldn't keep his eyes open. This part of the journey must have been torture to the cubs.

Dawn found us a few miles short of Namanga, close to the Tanganyika border. Here we allowed ourselves a brief rest and warmed ourselves with hot tea. The cubs were completely exhausted and lay apathetically in their cages, their faces chafed by the constant friction against the bars. The meat inside the crates was very high and covered with maggots, so we tried to remove it with iron scrapers which we had equipped ourselves with for the purpose, but the carcases had been so securely fastened to the bars that we could not move them. All we could do was to give the cubs fresh meat and water, in which they showed no interest.

To reduce the length of their misery as much as we could we decided that I should drive full speed ahead to Arusha, a hundred miles distant, announce our arrival to the Director of the National Parks, and find out the location of the release point in the Serengeti. (Because our move was taking place over a week-end, we had had no chance of sending a warning telegram.) George would follow with the cubs at a slower pace and we would meet at a short distance outside the town, where we should avoid a crowd of curious spectators.

It was a lovely morning, and I watched last night's clouds disperse, to disclose Mount Kilimanjaro rising above the early mist. Its cap of newly-fallen snow looked so ethereal in the soft morning light that it was difficult to believe that it was a glacier-crowned volcano. I have often admired Kilimanjaro from a distance, and I have climbed to its summit, but to-day more than ever it seemed a manifestation of glory, remote from the troubled world of man; part of the grandeur of an un-spoiled creation of which animals were an integral part. With this thought in my mind, I was sorry to see only three giraffe and a few impala antelope on plains where a few years ago wild life abounded. The increasing traffic along the new tar-mac road had driven the animals away, and I reflected that at the moment I myself was one of these destructive motorists; but at least my presence was justified by the hope of pro-viding the cubs with a natural life, unthreatened by man. I thought too that the length of time during which sanctuaries such as the national parks will be able to give refuge to wild animals will depend not only on the sympathy and active help of a few dedicated people, but on the support of all who live in Africa, whatever their race may be. This made me all the more determined to use the money, coming to me from the sale of books about Elsa and her cubs, to subsidise rescue teams to move doomed animals into sanctuaries or other preservation schemes. I hoped that the Elsa Appeal too would bring in more funds.

Approaching Arusha, I got a glimpse between shifting clouds of Mount Meru, and remembered that a friend of mine had seen a living rhino at a height of 15,000 feet on the rim of the crater of this conical volcano; whilst, at a height of 19,000 feet, at Gilman's point on Kilimanjaro the skeleton of a leopard had been found, and I had seen a buffalo skull some 16,000 feet at Mount Kenya. What, I wondered, had driven animals up to such forbidding heights?

As soon as I entered Arusha, I went to see the Director

of the National Parks. He was very friendly and welcomed the arrival of the cubs. I told him how grateful we were for the offer of sanctuary. He then asked me what we had done to inform the Press of the arrival of the cubs in the Serengeti. I replied that recently we had had no opportunity of contacting newspapermen, but that I was sure that they would by now have picked up the story. I added that, if he wished it, we would do our best to see that the hospitality given to the cubs by the Serengeti National Parks got the fullest publicity.

We then discussed the locality of the release point. I was surprised when he suggested Seronera as it is the H.Q. of the park and where all the park staff live. It is also a centre for tourists and a place at which planes, carrying visitors or provisions, frequently land. As we had always tried to preserve the cubs from human contacts, I pleaded for a more remote location, and the director agreed that we might take them farther afield to an area near a river which never went dry. He very kindly promised to send a radio message to one of the park wardens asking him to meet us on our way and guide us to this spot. He also offered us any further help we might need.

Before I left him the director presented me with a copy of the National Parks of Tanganyika Appeal. I explained, with some embarrassment, that all I had to give was going into the Elsa Appeal, adding that since wild animals everywhere needed help I personally felt that the more appeals there were the better. In the event, we both stuck loyally to our own Appeals.

After leaving the director it took me five hours' driving to find George who had driven the lorry 60 miles beyond Arusha. He explained that he had not been able to find any place nearer to Arusha which provided both shade and privacy. This was very inconvenient for it involved a serious delay—it meant that we should not be able to reach the Serengeti by nightfall. As the next stage of our journey was through highlands where it was bound to be very cold, we thought it would be unwise to continue, so we stopped at the foot of the Manyara Escarpment at about 3,500 altitude and camped at a small village called Mtu-ya-Umbu, Brook of the Mosquitoes, and it lived up to its name.

The cubs were in a pitiful state. Their faces were bruised and battered and the bony parts of their bodies were chafed; the decomposing meat inside the crates attracted a swarm of bluebottles which buzzed over their sores. They tried unsuccessfully to protect themselves by putting their paws over their faces; I could not bear to watch their suffering.

As the men were as tired as the rest of us, we decided not to pitch camp, and slept in the open. George and I put our beds close to the crates, and all through the night I heard the cubs moving about restlessly. At first light I roused the camp, which did not make me popular, but I was determined that the cubs should be released from their misery as soon as possible.

Soon, as we began to climb up the escarpment which towered above us, we saw Lake Manyara, until now hidden from our view by miles of virgin forest. This lake is one of the great attractions of Tanganyika. Its shallows are covered with flamingos and other water-fowl, while out of the lush forest elephant, buffalo and lion come to drink its waters.

We had no time to enjoy these sights for the sky was overcast and small showers warned us of more rain to come. Concentrating on speed, we climbed steadily into the ' Highlands of the Giant Volcanoes.' Unfortunately, drizzling rain reduced visibility to a few yards, so we were unable to see the volcanoes and Ngorongoro, the world's largest crater, which has a diameter of ten miles. We could only guess at the steep gradient of the slopes into which the road was cut by seeing, level with its verge, the tops of giant lobelias, a plant which grows to a height of nine feet.

The higher we climbed, the thicker the fog grew and it began to penetrate icily through our clothes. The men, who had never been at such a high altitude, looked blue under their dark African skins. Many droppings told us that this was not only a highway of tourists but also for buffalo, elephant and other wild beasts, and once an elephant stepped out of the thick bush and we had to stop abruptly.

At last we reached the rim of the crater. On an earlier visit, I had looked down it and seen a multitude of game grazing some 1,500 feet below, but to-day nothing was visible but billowing clouds. For a few miles we crawled cautiously along the slippery road round the rim, then, all of a sudden, the mist lifted; it was as though a curtain had suddenly been raised on a new scene and we saw, far below us, the Serengeti Plain bathed in warm sunlight.

Ahead of us lay undulating slopes, so profusely covered with bright yellow senecios that they might have been made of gold. Among this mass of flowers grazed great herds of zebra, wildebeest, Thomson's gazelle and cattle herded by Masai tribesmen. It was strange to see wild and domestic animals feeding side by side, a circumstance only made possible by the fact that the Masai do not poach ungulates.

We came down rapidly to an altitude of 5,000 feet, at which level the sun was so warm that we were able to shed some of our clothes. After passing the famous Olduvai Gorge, we knew that we now had only some seventy miles to go. The road had been fair so far; suddenly it deteriorated into one of the worst tracks we had ever travelled over. The ruts were knee-deep with lava dust, and rattling along them we stirred up a choking cloud which penetrated everything.

As the heat increased we removed the tarpaulins which covered the lorry, to prevent the cubs from suffocating, but this resulted in their raw wounds being covered with dust; they were indeed having a terrible time for they were bounced about mercilessly as the lorry lurched from one pothole to another. We had to stop often to jack the vehicles out of deep holes and replace broken springs. I did not know which was worse for the cubs, the icy wet and cold we had just left behind, or the infernal heat and appalling dust of the next fifty miles. We were two hours late when we reached Naabi Hill at which we were to meet the park warden; the poor man had spent the time watching our convoy creeping along like a caterpillar, raising a trial of dust in its wake.

Now we had to cut our greetings short, for heavy storm clouds were gathering and we still had a long way to go through black cotton soil, the worst ground to cross when wet. On our way we passed vast herds of wildebeeste and zebra; these were only the forerunners of the annual migration, but neither of us had ever before seen such an assembly of wild animals. Dodging between the herds and avoiding swampy patches we reached the release point in the late afternoon.

Chapter Thirteen

THE RELEASE

THE CUBS' NEW HOME was a very beautiful place lying at the head of a broad valley some forty miles long. On one side, a steep escarpment rose to a plateau, on the other, there was a succession of hills. Close by, was a river which gradually wound its way to the centre of the valley and flowed down it. Its banks were covered with dense undergrowth and fine trees, which provided perfect cover for all kinds of animals. The valley looked like a park, with clusters of thorn trees and bush which higher up the hills increased in density. But for the mosquitoes and tsetse flies, it was a paradise—and perhaps we ought to have regarded the tsetse as its winged guardians, for they are the best protectors of wild animals : since they are fatal to men and to their livestock, they cause them to keep away. The warden did not wish to become benighted on his way home for it is against the park rules to drive in the dark, so when he had suggested a good camping site he left us.

Our first thought was to see what we could do to make the cubs more comfortable. We chose a stout acacia tree, attached the block and tackle to one of its branches, and swung the crates to the ground. It was three days since the cubs had been captured and they had almost reached the limit of their endurance. Their eyes were deeply sunken and they lay apathetically on the floor of their cages, apparently too tired to take the least interest in their surroundings. How glad we were that we had decided to bring the cumbersome communal crate. It had no floor, could easily be moved to fresh ground, and would provide the lions with a spacious and comfortable place of confinement in which they would be able to recover from the strain of their journey.

After opening the back of the communal crate, we placed

Little Elsa's and Gopa's boxes with their doors opposite the opening, then with block and tackle we raised the trapdoors of the cages.

For a few moments nothing happened, then, suddenly, Gopa rushed into Little Elsa's box; he sat on her and they licked and hugged each other, overwhelmed with joy at being reunited. Quickly we closed the door behind them and replaced Gopa's empty crate by the one containing Jespah. The instant we opened his door he was out like a flash, and covered his brother and sister, as if to protect them from further disaster and started to lick and embrace them.

As we watched them we became more than ever convinced that we had done well to move the cubs in crates which allowed them to see each other. This had probably resulted in some extra chafing, but it would be easier to heal wounds than broken spirits. We were delighted to see that in spite of all they had gone through the cubs were as friendly as they had always been. If we had been able to give them tranquillisers we could probably have avoided the chafing, but as we had to move them in such improvised conditions we had no means of administering the Librium and we had been warned against using drugs which might have lowered their resistance and retarded their recovery.

Now we had to see that they got rested and made up for their lost meals. We put a carcase into the communal crate, told our men to camp a little way off and parked our Land-Rovers right and left of the crate to protect the cubs from any prowlers that might come by night.

By 9 p.m. all this had been done, and we were ready for a good sleep. But Gopa soon became restless and often during the night I heard him shifting about, and the crunching of bones. Next morning I was glad to see that there was nothing left of the meal we had prepared the night before. The cubs had gone back into the filthy travelling crates; they seemed to cling to them as the one familiar place which gave them a sense of security in their strange surroundings. As a result we were unable to remove the rotten meat.

Until they became less bewildered it was plain that we must

keep them confined; to entice them into the communal crate we put some fresh meat into it. We thought it very important to leave them undisturbed, so we gave strict orders to our staff to keep away from the crates, and we ourselves went to find a camping site at least a mile away. After pitching our tents we came back and saw that the cubs had not moved out of their dirty cages which were buzzing with flies. Ignoring their protests we cleaned out the crates as best we could. It was not an easy task, for the cubs defended their little territory, growling and scratching. Both George and I were sick several times as we scraped out the filth, so when the repulsive operation was completed, we went back to camp to have a bath and the first hot meal we had eaten for four days.

While we were eating the park warden and his family came to discuss our camping arrangements. The park authorities had kindly given us permission to look after the cubs until they had settled in their new home and could fend for themselves. The park warden told us that we could feed them on game animals shot outside the Serengeti Park, specified the area, which was some 40 miles away, and also the type of animal we were allowed to shoot. He offered us any help we might need, was very sympathetic and stayed with us until late in the afternoon.

When we got back to the cubs we found all three in the communal crate. Their faces were a shocking sight, for the big cage was made of weld-mesh wire which chafed them even more than the iron bars of the travelling crates. Every time they pressed against it their wounds reopened, and they made matters worse by using their paws to try and keep the flies off their sores. Poor Gopa was the most battered and he and Little Elsa growled savagely whenever we came close to the crate. Jespah did not mind our presence and even allowed us to pluck at the arrowhead; but we failed to extract it.

We settled down for the night, the communal cage sheltered between our two cars; soon afterwards we heard the first lion approaching. The whuffing came rapidly nearer, until we could distinguish several animals circling round our little sanctuary—and then saw their eyes reflecting the light of our torches. The cubs listened intently to their grunts, while we shouted at them trying to shoo them away. When all was quiet again, I called the cubs softly by their names, and soon afterwards heard them tearing at their meat. I was disturbed to notice that one of them was breathing heavily and I feared it might be going to develop pneumonia. But when it became light I was pleased to see that, in spite of the heavy dew, none of the cubs seemed to be seriously ill—in fact they looked very content and their bellies were full.

It was a brisk, fresh morning; even at this altitude—about 3,500 feet—the lowest in the Serengeti, the air was much cooler than at Elsa's camp. In the evening we had covered the crate with a tarpaulin; now we removed it as the sun was rising. As soon as it got hot the horrid flies appeared and literally covered the cubs. Poor Jespah kept brushing one front paw against his sores, while with the other he hugged Little Elsa.

After breakfast, George drove off to shoot a 'kill' outside the Serengeti while I remained with the cubs. Whenever he gave me an opportunity to do so I tried to remove the arrow from Jespah's rump. He did not mind even when I pinched the skin and tugged as hard as I could, but the barb remained jammed. Jespah had been hit five weeks ago and I did not like the look of the wound; but as the vet had advised against operating for a few more weeks, I had to resign myself to waiting.

Later in the morning the plague of flies made the cubs very restless; they paced up and down, rubbing their heads against the wire and reopening their wounds, but in the end cuddled up together, looking at me reproachfully. It spite of being caged, dirty and covered with bleeding wounds, they were as dignified as only lions could be under such conditions.

I knew that the Serengeti was far the best home we could have found for them, but the climate and the ecological conditions were very different from those of their old home and most of the local animals belonged to species unknown to them. Even the local lions were of a different sub-species from theirs. What would their mutual reactions be and what trouble might arise over territorial rights? Since there was so much game about that every animal could be assured of an ample food supply, I could only hope that the lions of the Serengeti were more tolerant than the Fierce Lioness who had attacked Elsa.

All that morning I stayed close to the crate, refilling the cod-liver oil and water containers whenever they were emptied. Now, the first time for several months, I was able to observe the cubs closely. One thing I noticed was that Little Elsa's canine teeth were almost three times as large as those of her brothers, and I wondered whether this was an individual characteristic or only the normal ratio of development between the sexes. Since it is the lioness who usually does the killing, it seems possible that she develops stronger canines at an earlier age than the male, and that this is more obvious at puberty than when the animals are mature. But to establish the fact one would need to make a comparative study of the skulls of lions of both sexes during puberty.

When George returned about 3 o'clock with a carcase we discussed the question of releasing the cubs. We had intended to keep them confined for another day or two so as to build them up, but the torment of the flies made us change our minds and we decided to release them then and there.

It was a good time of day, since during the hot hours the cubs were less energetic, therefore less likely to bolt or panic; moreover, at this hour there was less danger of their meeting wild lions. After placing the carcase between the cage and the river, we hoisted one of the travelling boxes, thus opening an exit. When they saw us doing this the cubs rushed in terror to the farthest corners of the communal crate and huddled close together. After some time, Gopa suspiciously investigated the opening, cautiously retreated several times, and then walked out in a most dignified manner. He took no interest in the 'kill' but continued slowly towards the river. After about a hundred yards he stopped, hesitated, and then walked calmly on.

Jespah and Little Elsa held each other close; they had puzzled expressions as they watched Gopa walking away. Then Jespah went up to the exit and moved out. He too went very slowly towards the river, pausing several times to look back at his sister.

Meanwhile Little Elsa rushed frantically up and down the crate or stood upright against it, plainly desperately anxious to join her brothers and not knowing how to do so, till at last she found the way to freedom and trotted quickly after Jespah, and all three cubs disappeared into the reeds. Almost immediately a cloudburst screened them from our view.

Chapter Fourteen

THE MIGRATION

As soon as the grey curtain lifted we searched the place where we had last seen the cubs through our field-glasses but there was no trace of them. I was glad that at least they had walked straight to the river, since this meant that they would know where to get a drink.

Although the river was not so lovely as the one at Elsa's camp, it provided for all the cubs' needs; its bed carried a slow-flowing stream of fresh water, and even in the dry season a few pools, milky and stagnant, would remain; and beyond the far bank a chain of hills concealed an extensive salt-lick which was frequented by many animals. We were happy to think that if only our cubs were accepted by the local lions they were not going to find life too difficult here.

To avoid quarrels one of our first tasks would be to find a feeding place, where the cubs could eat without the local lions or other predators interfering with them. To secure their meat inside the communal crate would be risky, for in a confined space the cubs might be cornered. What we needed was a shelter for the 'kill' which provided an easy exit for the cubs in case of danger. We placed the communal crate near a large tree; on either side we parked our two cars, thus making an open square. Across a thick branch we hoisted the 'kill' by a block and tackle, which we attached to one of the cars; this would make it easy to lower the meat during the night if the cubs appeared, and while they were absent the carcase would dangle out of reach of thieves. We did not expect the cubs that night, for until they were hungry we did not think they would return to the crates in which they had been trapped.

Soon after dark a pride of three or more lions came so close that the light from our torches was reflected in their eyes. They

were followed by a few hyenas. A little later we heard
baboons shrieking in alarm, and sweeping our spotlight in the
direction from which the noise came saw three pairs of eyes,
half-way up the hill beyond the river. We thought these
might be those of the cubs who, after their experience with
the Fierce Lioness, were likely to keep away from other lions.

To discourage the wild pride from coming to get a free
meal, we spent most of the night scaring them away. It was
easy to know when the lion was around for he always announced his arrival by a low grunt, but the lionesses sneaked
in silently and I only became aware of them when I heard
the breathing and by then they were crouching by my car.
However, in spite of their cunning they never got at the ' kill.'

Early next morning we screened the river banks through our
field-glasses, but saw no sign of the cubs. It was only when the
first rays of the sun touched the water that we spotted them
coming out of the bush, very close to the place at which they
had disappeared the night before. They walked half-way up
the hill, stopping often, until they reached a thicket; there
they lay down. When I called to them they looked at me but
did not move. Then a troop of baboons came in sight, and
the cubs walked at a leisurely pace to the top of the hill with
the baboons close behind them. Finally the whole party disappeared over the crest.

Hoping to be able to follow the cubs' movements, we drove
across the river and along the far side of the hill, but we did
not see them. On our way we were overtaken by a Land-
Rover which had brought a radiogram saying that our new
Bedford was now ready and could be collected at Nairobi.
Mail in the Serengeti was dependent on occasional transport,
but telegrams were transmitted twice daily by radio from
Arusha H.Q.

We sent Ibrahim to Nairobi to return the truck, which Ker
and Downey had so kindly hired us at a low price; he was to
bring back the Bedford.

Next evening the cubs arrived at about 9 p.m. They ate
hungrily but when George switched on his headlights, bolted
and did not return for an hour. This time they settled down

to their dinner. Jespah even asked for two rations of cod-liver oil and took it in his usual way out of the pie-dish which George held out to him, so we knew that in spite of all he had lately suffered he still trusted us.

In the early hours of the morning I heard one of the cubs moving towards the river; it gave a series of short roars, but I noticed that these were not followed by the whuffs with which a lion's roar should end.

Little Elsa made the most of her brother's absence and ate heartily at the kill. Later, all three cubs had a good fill-up for the day and left at dawn. As soon as they had gone a lion roared loudly; he was alarmingly close and soon I saw a splendid dark-maned lion clearly silhouetted against the blood-red morning sky. He sniffed in the direction of the kill, then walked to the back of George's car and watched the mosquito-net flapping inside. When he showed an inclination to in-vestigate the carcase, we shouted at the top of our voices, and though we couldn't compete with his roars we did succeed in startling him and he trotted off in the direction of the camp. As soon as he had gone, we hoisted the kill beyond his reach and then drove to the camp to warm ourselves with some hot tea.

When we got there we saw this dark-maned lion standing within a hundred yards of the excited boys who, from their refuge on top of the lorry, were trying to warn us of his presence. Poor lion, he must have wondered what to make of such an unexpected invasion of his territory.

We spent the day reconnoitring the area. The annual mig-ration of the animals of the plain was expected to move through the valley soon, but, although the day before George had seen some large herds of wildebeeste and zebra assembling near the border, to-day we saw only the usual inhabitants of the valley: herds of impala, topi, waterbuck and kongoni and some solitary bushbuck and reedbuck and later, as we went farther down the valley, many buffalo and a few elephant.

Towards evening we went back to our post near the 'kill.' Gopa arrived at dusk, but hid in the tall grass until he thought it was dark enough to be safe for him to come to his meal.

Jespah soon followed him, but Little Elsa did not appear. Instead, the dark-maned lion and his two lionesses turned up. They crouched within eight yards of my car while, on the other side of it, Gopa and Jespah crunched their dinner. I was sorry I had not got a flashlight and could not take a photograph of this absurd party; three hungry wild lions crouching in the grass, only separated from the cubs by my car. Jespah and Gopa were not in the least worried by the proximity of the local lions, indeed, they must have felt perfectly safe and have had complete confidence in our ability to protect them, for when they were full up they rolled on their backs.

Suddenly there was a faint call from over the river; perhaps it was Little Elsa for instantly the brothers sneaked off behind George's car, avoiding the wild lions. We hoisted the kill and spent the rest of the night keeping the wild pride at bay.

On the 7th of May, George left early to get a new 'kill' outside the Serengeti. The track to the border was rough and I did not expect him back till the afternoon. About lunch-time the clouds gathered threateningly over the camp; as the first drops fell a Land-Rover unexpectedly appeared, bringing the Chairman of the Trustees of the National Park and his party, which included the park warden. We hurried into the tent to avoid a drenching. The chairman told me that he appreciated the publicity the cubs were giving to the Serengeti, but went on to say that by the end of May we must leave, as the tourist season opened in June and our camping out and feeding the lions might arouse criticism. I was horrified, for we had brought the cubs to the Serengeti believing that we should be allowed to look after them until they were able to provide for themselves, and no one could yet tell when that would be. I told the chairman that we had always wished to ensure that the cubs should eventually lead a wild life, and that for this reason we had refrained from making pets of them; but I stressed that we really could not abandon them until they were able to fend for themselves. I suggested, to avoid the difficulties he foresaw, that we should move our camp to some place far from the tourist tracks, and I promised to be very discreet about feeding the cubs, but pointed out that by the end of May they would only be seventeen months old and that as a rule lions of that age are not yet able to hunt on their own.

At this moment George returned, and supported my view. The chairman did not agree to our proposal and left us dismayed. The cubs had only been released a few days; up till then they had been dependent upon us, and we felt it would be monstrous just to dump them and hope that they would manage somehow.

We were still discussing the situation when more visitors arrived. These included Lee and Matty Talbot, American scientists engaged in ecological research. Their views were most stimulating, they shared many of our interests and we soon became friends.

When we took up our night station we found the cubs already waiting for us. George was tired after his long drive, so he went to sleep and I sat up to guard the cubs. Jespah came several times to the back of my car asking to be patted and remained quite still while I stroked him. This was the first time he had done such a thing since he had left Elsa's camp. In spite of all that had happened, perhaps because of his mother's example, he still trusted us and acted as liaison between his brother and sister and ourselves. We were both sure that without him neither Gopa nor Little Elsa would have put up with us. Gopa had the strength and independence to be the leader of a pride, but he lacked the qualities of affection and understanding which distinguished his mother and his brother. Although it was Gopa who left the Tana, made his way back to his old home and spent a week there on his own; although he was the one to fight most fiercely when he was trapped and who first took the risk of making his way to freedom out of the communal crate and claimed the lion's share of every meal—yet, when he was distressed or frightened, Gopa at once rushed to Jespah for comfort and support, as he used to rush to his mother.

Jespah appeared to provide the moral backbone for the trio, which was probably what caused him to become the leader, even though he was less powerful than Gopa. From a very early age he had always protected his mother and since her death he had taken charge of his brother and sister. It was always he who went out to reconnoitre and see if there was danger around, and if a threat arose it was he who challenged it and recently whenever Little Elsa bolted he had run after her, comforted her and brought her back.

The cubs spent the night devouring the fresh kill. At dawn they walked off, their bellies swinging heavily from side to side. They were in perfect condition, except for some sores from chafing, and of course Jespah still had the arrowhead in his rump.

During the next two nights only the three local lions and a few hyena came to the kill. One of these was particularly cunning. He waited beyond the range of our headlights until we were no longer on the alert and then dashed up to the meat.

There was no sign of the cubs and as my injured leg still prevented me from taking long walks, George went off alone to search for them. He found their spoor leading across the valley towards the escarpment, where rocks offered them good shelter. We thought that they probably felt safer at a distance from the local lions, even if this meant that they had to walk two miles to get their dinner.

One afternoon we drove across the plain to look at some rocky outcrops which provided ideal lie-ups for lions. Gigantic boulders, piled haphazard upon each other, formed cliffs, caves, crevasses and platforms, all of which were overgrown by a jungle of shrub whose silvery roots gripped the rocks like tentacles. It was a splendid landscape, the candelabra-shaped branches of the grey-green euphorbias stood out against a deep blue sky, while in the chaos of stone and vegetation the red blossoms of aloes gleamed like rubies. These picturesque islands rose above a flat plain in which Thomson's gazelle, wildebeeste, topi, zebra and kongoni were peacefully grazing, and ostriches strutted among them, hardly any of which bothered to raise their heads as we drove by.

As we passed some rocks we saw a pride of lions, who sleepily observed our approach but soon lost interest in us and continued their siesta. They were lying in the shade of a fig-tree whose roots seemed to grow out of sheer rock, and were huddled so close together that it took us some time before we discovered that the tawny heap consisted of three lionesses and five cubs. Two of the cubs could not have been more than three weeks old; the others were about the same age as Elsa's cubs; though they were smaller their ruffs were much longer than those of Jespah and Gopa. Young lions are most endearing for they still retain the puzzled inquisitive expression of small cubs, while they already have the dignity and stateliness of adult lions.

Two of the lionesses were obviously the mothers of the cubs; the third we assumed to be the traditional 'aunt.' Tumbling clumsily over the bodies of their elders, the two tiny cubs dominated the scene. One, struggling up towards its mother's shoulders, miaouwed in protest when it got stuck, then clambered on, only to roll over and land on Auntie's back, from which vantage point it seized the black tassel at the end of her tail. A quick flick sent it scurrying up her neck, till it found two ears, which it started to chew. But no aunt, however tolerant, could be expected to put up with such impertinence, and this one, shaking her massive head, sent the little cub flying. Hurriedly it scrambled over to its mother, pressing itself against her soft belly, suckling for all it was worth.

Looking at the older cubs, I wished that Elsa's could join such a happy family, but I feared that they were already too big to be adopted by a pride; on the other hand, they might be at a good age to start off on their own life, for since they were still too young to compete with adult lions for a mate they ought not to get involved in any serious quarrels in the next few months, during which they could learn the art of hunting. Three lions were enough to form a competent pride, though it might be hard for Little Elsa to be the mate of two lions.

That night the cubs arrived soon after our vigil had begun. They seemed unusually nervous and bolted the moment they heard a lion calling, even though he was far away. They did not return till three in the morning, then gulped their food and left. We appreciated the reason for the hurry when soon afterwards a chorus of lions started to roar quite close to us.

On the following night the same thing happened, and Little Elsa was in such a state of nerves that she even bolted when we used our torches.

When, in the morning, Ibrahim arrived with the new Bedford it gave me a pang to see ELSA LTD. painted on its door. This lorry which was to be used by the first rescue team financed by the royalties from Elsa's book, was to go into operation as soon as the cubs had established themselves. I only hoped it might be used to move many animals to safety in conditions a lot more comfortable than those which Elsa's cubs had endured on their journey to the Serengeti.

It rained all day and we went early to the ' kill.' When we reached it we saw Jespah balancing on the branch from which his dinner was hanging; he was trying to get at it from above, while the other cubs, half hidden in the grass, watched him. As soon as we lowered the carcase they all rushed at the meat and spent the night gorging. By morning there was nothing left but a few bones; this meant that we must again drive outside the Serengeti and go hunting for them.

Quite close to the camp we passed the dark-maned lion and his two girl friends. We had always supposed that lions like to pass their honeymoon in privacy and were therefore surprised to see this lion making love to one of the lionesses in the presence of the other. Not more than a mile farther on we saw a magnificent blond-maned lion sunning himself on the open plain. He paid no attention to us or to the clicking of our cameras and stretched and yawned as though we weren't there. After that, I had hardly time to change my film before we ran into another pair of lovesick lions. They lay as close together as they could, seemed very tired, and ignored us.

The plain was glistening from the night's rain, each blade of grass sparkled with drops of dew. In whatever direction we looked we saw animals chasing and fighting each other. The cheeky little Thomson's gazelle not only challenged each

The Tana in flood

The cubs were like skeletons when George found them on the Tana

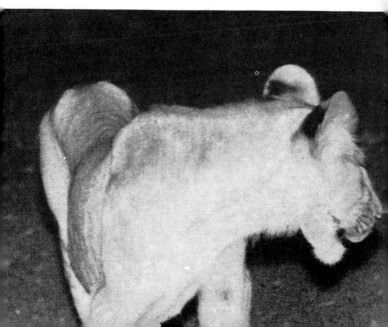

George's device with the three cages for trapping the cubs simultaneously

A rhinoceros under Kilimanjaro, Amboseli Game Reserve

Jespah in his crate

The cubs recovering from the journey

Jespah at the end of the journey—note the arrow-head

George opens a travelling box to let the cubs into the communal crate

Release!

The ravine in which the cubs settled and where we fed them

other to a game, but even our Land-Rover. At our approach they stamped their forelegs, but did not move away until we nearly bumped into them. Then eland-antelopes, larger than bulls, bounded away so gracefully that one could have imagined that their heavy bodies were weightless, and troops of mongoose, who had been basking in the sun on top of ant-hills, scampered into the grass or dived into air-funnels. Comic-looking kongoni frolicked amongst herds of topi, which tossed their black heads and snorted as if they were blowing their noses, and some sleek silver-backed jackals, watching a hobbling hyena searching for food, peeped out from between tufts of grass.

The farther we drove, the more wooded and hilly the country became and the more the herds of animals increased. When we neared the border we might have been passing a gigantic cattle sale such as the stock-rearing tribes hold on the northern frontier. Mile after mile under every tree groups of wildebeeste and zebra crowded together to the limit of the shade; whilst, in the blazing sun, animals unable to find shelter wandered about aimlessly. The noise was deafening. When I closed my eyes I might have been listening to a chorus of bullfrogs, and only the high-pitched barking of the zebra reminded me that we were not in a swamp but amongst thousands upon thousands of animals assembled in preparation for their great annual migration towards Lake Victoria and the adjoining Mara Reserve. We were very lucky to have arrived in the Serengeti in time to see this unique sight. In 1958 the Grzimeks started to make a census from the air of these migratory plain animals, and now a second census, in which the Wilken Air Services, Wild Life Research Project U.S.A., the Fauna Research Unit of the Kenya Game De-partment and Tanganyika National Parks were co-operating, was taking place. As we drove along we heard the vibration of an aircraft and saw it circling low as the observers took their count. Months later, when I asked for the result of this survey I was given the following staggering figures of heads counted. These figures were said to be a conservative estimate, and the Serengeti is only 5,400 square miles.

F.F.   E

Thomson's Gazelle	500,000
Wildebeeste	221,699
Zebra	151,006
Buffalo	15,898
Topi	15,766
Eland	2,450
Kongoni	1,379
Elephant	720
Rhino	29

It was suggested that the number of lion might be between 300 and 400, but as they are rarely seen from aircraft no very reliable figure could be recorded.

When we returned to the cubs' feeding place with our 'kill,' we found Jespah and Gopa doing acrobatics along the branches of the acacia tree above their dinner and Little Elsa hiding nearby. Suddenly Gopa listened in her direction, and began to scramble down. When he had nearly reached the ground he jumped and fell heavily; then he got to his feet, looking rather foolish, and trotted over to his sister. Jespah remained on his branch till I showed him the pie-dish, then he too came down and almost toppled over in his eagerness to get at the cod-liver oil. I was glad to see that his sores were nearly healed and that a fine fluff was growing over the scars, but the wound made by the arrowhead was discharging and looked very nasty.

We had recently discussed with our ecologist friend, Lee Talbot, whether or not to try to operate on Jespah. He was against giving the cub the drugs necessary to anæsthetise him and thought that we should wait a little longer to see if the arrowhead might not slough out of itself.

When it was quite dark Little Elsa came to the meat, but seemed terribly nervous, so I tried to reassure her by calling her name. Later we did our best to scare off the wild lions and hyenas but in spite of this the cubs left and did not return.

After breakfast we went off to see more of the migration. On our way we passed the mating lion and his lioness again. Although they were lying in the open and must have seen us, they allowed us to approach to within twenty-five yards of them, and were so little disturbed by our arrival that eventually the lion sired his mate; an act which lasted three minutes and ended by his giving her a gentle bite on the forehead to which she responded with a low growl. After a quarter of an hour he approached her again, but this time she dismissed him with a sweep of her paw. This was repeated three times before she permitted him to sire her again and, as before, he bit her forehead. We continued to watch them, and after about twenty minutes the lion sired her a third time releasing her only after giving her a slight bite in the neck; after this both went to sleep. There was no sound to be heard and time seemed to stand still on this vast plain. When we started up the car, the lioness raised her head and blinked at us through half-closed eyes, but the lion never stirred.

We had been told that in the Serengeti there were many more lionesses than lions. This no doubt accounted for the un-usual number of love-making pairs we saw. Lions nearly always keep a harem, and can manage a large family success-fully since a lioness spends two years looking after her cubs and does not allow herself to be sired during this time. But here, the males being vastly outnumbered by females, a good many of the lions we saw looked rather thin. We thought this was partly because a lion's honeymoon usually lasts four or five days, and during this time the couple do not eat and seldom drink, and here there were not enough lions to satisfy the demand of so many lionesses, so the lions often went hungry. The reason given for the preponderance of females was that since the Serengeti lions are famous for their ex-ceptionally fine manes, when they venture outside the park they are often killed by hunters. Over the border, in the Ikoma area in one year alone (1959/60) eighty-eight lions were shot. A year later the Tanganyika Game Department decided to issue only six licences to shoot lion along the border. This area is of course outside the competence of the National Parks Committee.

Soon after we got back to camp the Director of the National Parks came to see us. He asked us to pay £100, the fee for taking commercial photographs or films within the park. Saying that the money raised by my books was earmarked for subsidising game preservation schemes did not relieve us of the obligation to conform to the park rules applicable to commercial photography. We were also asked to present the lodge at Seronera with two enlargements of photographs of the cubs to be used as publicity for the national park.

During the next three nights the cubs failed to turn up, but hungry predators were very active. A leopard climbed the acacia tree in an attempt to get at the meat; a bold hyena also tried his luck, and several lions came to investigate the 'kill.' In particular, the dark-maned lion and his pride remained close and were plainly not prepared to allow the cubs to take over their territory.

This made us realise that we must establish a new feeding place for the cubs—but first we had to find them. Our knowledge of the territorial habits of lions was based on what happened in the N.F.D. (Northern Frontier District). There the two man-eaters of Merti had ranged over fifty miles and allowed no rivals in their area, and the Fierce Lioness who occasionally visited Elsa's camp, had covered over thirty miles on her rounds and even if she shared her hunting ground with other lions in rotation, all stuck to a routine which kept the area well stocked with game. In every case the lions of the N.F.D. had been conservative in their habits and territorial claims. But here, with such a quantity of lions and such a wealth of game, territorial rights were difficult to assess.

We were told that during the season of the migration many lions simply followed the column of moving animals, since they found it easier to kill stragglers than to hunt in the usual way. All we could hope to do was to discover where the more conservative prides had established their rights and remove our cubs to another area.

We spent the next days scouring the country, but the long grass and dry ground made spooring difficult. Besides this, there were so many lions in the valley that it was impossible to identify the cubs' pug marks.

Once again we saw an impala ram staring intently at a bush,

behind which three cubs were crouching, but they were not ours. Suddenly their mother started to stalk the impala, who only escaped thanks to our interference. There were innumerable birds in this area and we were often guided to kills by circling vultures. More attractive were the flocks of green and orange lovebirds which displayed their dazzling plumage.

As for lions, we had never seen so many : we walked past a pride of five sitting on a rock, and a short distance away from them we saw a pride of seven lying on a hillock, who looked us up and down but didn't move, even when we had to pass within four yards of them. As we went on we came upon a third pride consisting of a lioness, two small cubs, two half-grown cubs and two magnificent lions, and only a short distance away two dark-maned lions were stalking a topi up a hill; as it was getting hot and they were not very enthusiastic he got away. Later we were several times surprised to see two fully-grown lions together but were told that in the Serengeti a pair of lions will sometimes remain together for many years. How different is the behaviour of the lions of the Serengeti from that of those we knew in the N.F.D.

We went to a small lake to watch the flamingos who were standing on its edge and noticed a hammer-headed stork pecking at its food in the shallows, close to a sleeping monitor. The lizard was rather a large specimen, about four feet long. As we were looking at it a jackal approached the monitor from behind—obviously not with the best intentions. We had been told of jackals eating puff-adders, and of lions around Lake Rudolf killing crocodiles, but neither George nor I had ever seen a carnivore kill and eat a reptile. The monitor seemed completely unaware of danger until the jackal was near enough to make a bite at him, then he lashed his tail threateningly and his attacker leapt into the air and bolted. The monitor went to sleep again, but the jackal was not to be put off so easily. He returned to the attack this time approaching the monitor from the front. He was greeted by a loud hiss, which sent him dashing off into the grass, where a lioness suddenly sat up in front of him, her two cubs peeping out to right and left of her and the jackal nearly fell backwards in his hurry to be off. Seeing this the lioness strolled to the water and began to drink quite close to the monitor, who waddled away very quickly. None of this disturbed the hammer-headed stork, who went on pecking industriously, completely disregarding lion, jackal and monitor.

When the cubs had been missing for six days we became anxious. We had expected them to become independent only gradually, and this sudden disappearance didn't seem natural. We wondered whether they might share the homing instinct with cats. If so, they might now be travelling to their old homes—400 miles if they went in a straight line; 700 if they followed the route by which they had come. That they should follow the road seemed unlikely, but we decided to investigate it and drove back thirty miles to the hill, to where we had first met the park warden. We saw no sign of the cubs. On our way we passed through vast herds of migrating animals and saw one column three miles long of Thomson's gazelle walking in single file, advancing as if drawn by a magnet. In spite of the easy hunting, we did not think it probable that the cubs would have gone into this country, for the open plain offered no shelter and they were used to thick bush cover. All the same, we made a careful search in the rocks and vegetation of the hill before we gave up and returned to camp.

The next morning we took a map and drew a straight line between the Serengeti and Elsa's camp.

As soon as it left the Serengeti the line entered an area inhabited by the Masai tribe which is noted for lion hunting. Before the time of the European administration each young warrior of this tribe was obliged, in order to prove his manhood, to spear a lion, whose mane he converted into a headdress which he thereafter wore on special occasions as a proof of his courage. Lion spearing was now forbidden by the game laws but still went on secretly, so we did not think that we should count on getting news of our cubs in this area. We therefore thought of sending Makedde who, though himself a Turkana, could speak Masai, to camp among the tribesmen and see whether in casual conversation he could pick up any news of the cubs. If they had raided stock he would perhaps be able to prevent them from being speared.

On our way to the border we stopped at Seronera to call on the director, who was staying there, and tell him of our plans. He said he was sorry that we had run into difficulties, but made it clear that we should be obliged to leave the Serengeti by the end of the month whatever the position might be by then. This left us only ten days, an alarmingly short time.

We passed through some country where there was plenty of cover, but also plenty of lions. We saw a pride of fifteen lying under a tree. Two males with splendid manes watched over their families, consisting of five lionesses who were suckling eight cubs of varying ages. The cubs went from one mother to the other, and the lionesses showed no wish to distinguish between their own cubs and the others.

It was late afternoon when we reached the border, so there was no time left to find a Masai manyatta (boma) where Makedde might find hospitality. We therefore decided to return for the night and planned that next morning I should drive Makedde and his kit into the Masai area and try to find a family who would take him in, while George would go on searching the valley near the camp.

As soon as we got back I packed, to be ready for an early start; then I went to the cubs' feeding place to spend the night there in case they might come. Since we had so little time left, George decided to start searching the valley at once. Next morning he arrived grinning; he had found the cubs, or rather they had found him.

He had driven six miles down the valley and parked the car where the headlights could be seen over a great distance and at intervals he had flashed the spotlight to all the points of the compass.

About 9 p.m. the cubs arrived. They looked fit and were not hungry, but they were so thirsty that the brothers lapped up all the water George could give them, leaving nothing for poor Little Elsa. All were very friendly and Jespah even tried to enter George's car. They remained there through the night, eating little of the very high meat he had brought them but amusing themselves by chasing hyenas. When, soon after dawn, they left, they went towards a little valley. George had hurried back to bring me the good news and stopped me going to the border. It was obvious that, after their experience with the Fierce Lioness at Elsa's camp home, the cubs were scared of all the lions round the release place and had gone to find a more secluded area where they could stake out their own territory.

We decided not to move the main camp but to go every evening to the ' cub valley ' and spend the night there in our cars. The glen they had chosen for their home was at the foot of the escarpment and above the tsetse belt, it was about a mile and a half long and two narrow ravines led into and out of it. One of these provided a particularly safe refuge. It was about half a mile long, its vertical walls were nine feet high and it was five feet wide; above it almost impenetrable vegetation provided a thick canopy which turned it into a cool shelter during the hot hours of the day.

Any approaching danger could be heard from a long way off, so, if need be, the cubs could retreat inside the ravine and up one of the sheer cliffs which broke off the escarpment. Here among over-hanging rocks and dense undergrowth they would be in a strong strategic position to sight and avoid an enemy. From the top of the escarpment there was a splendid view across the vast, undulating hinterland of woods and parkland to the river, another valley through which it ran and beyond it to hills and other valleys which stretched out to the horizon. The course of the river was marked by a green belt which wound along the valley till it was lost in a haze. We thought that the cubs had found a much better home for themselves than the one we had chosen for them.

When we first arrived at their valley it was late afternoon, we took up our post under a large tree between the escarpment and the river and hoisted up the meat. One cub soon emerged from the ravine but hid in the grass. When it grew dark all three appeared and went straight to the water bowl. They were very thirsty and we had to refill the basin many times before they were satisfied. We observed that all three were in good condition, and the sores due to the chafing were healing well. The arrowhead in Jespah's rump, however, showed no sign of coming out and though he drank his cod-liver oil from the pie-dish I held out to him he would not allow me to pull at the arrow. When they had quenched their thirst the cubs went off into the darkness and did not come back for their supper until George switched off the headlights of the car. We realised they had not changed their purely nocturnal habits and in general only appeared at night and left at dawn.

Chapter Fifteen

THE RAVINE

As soon as we had found the cubs George sent the news to Seronera.

Later that day we met the director and on the following afternoon he came to our camp, and we discussed the cubs' future with him. He suggested that we should now go away and leave them to their fate, but when we argued that they were not yet able to fend for themselves and that we were worried about Jespah's arrow wound, he agreed that we should stay on until the end of May to help them.

That evening Jespah and Gopa came from the ravine at dusk, but Little Elsa did not appear. Gopa tore greedily at the meat while Jespah went back to his sister and the two of them remained outside the range of the lights until George turned them out, when they came up and joined Gopa.

Next day we went to have another look at the migration; it was a truly fantastic sight. The migrating herds spend several weeks assembling; during this time they churn up the plain and after a couple of days the three-foot high grass is reduced to bare stalks of only about four inches. The actual move lasts only a few days and its drive and urgency is something which has to be seen to be believed. What mysterious force suddenly informs these usually placid animals and causes them to move as if at a command? Can it be only a search for water and for better pasturing? These are certainly important factors and ecological research has proved how dependent animals are on certain species of grass and the extent to which they are prepared to abandon their usual territorial habits in order to find them, but these factors alone seem inadequate to explain the vast simultaneous movement. Surely some deeper atavism inherited perhaps from bygone ages must be responsible for the phenomenon.

How, otherwise, is it possible to explain the suicidal migration of the lemmings? They move only at night when its difficult for them to find the lichens and grasses on which they feed, and when they reach the sea, they plunge into it and drown.

We watched in amazement the herds advancing in tens of thousands and sometimes had the impression that it was the ground itself that was moving. The wildebeeste kept in groups of ten to one hundred or walked in single file along well trodden paths, the zebra, whenever possible, kept close to the water; these two species predominated, but there were also great herds of Thomson's gazelles, also many smaller ones of Grant's gazelles, kongoni and topi, and we counted one herd of two hundred eland-antelopes. On the periphery of the herds were hungry jackals and hyenas watching for the chance to pick up a straggler. In whatever direction we looked the plain was covered with animals whose number it was impossible to estimate.

During the cool hours they were full of energy. We were particularly amused by the behaviour of the shaggy wildebeeste. The bulls chased any of their cows which strayed off, and challenged rivals to a fight, while the cows tossed their heads and kicked out with their hooves at too persistent suitors. Many times an 'army' of them passed by, covering us with dust. I became very anxious for our cameras, so I covered them up and in consequence got no pictures. Once a herd of many hundred zebras galloped past our car, their thundering hooves stirring up a pall of dust; when they had almost passed by, through the cloud of dust I saw a lion leaping upon the last of the zebras; he missed his prey and so did a second lion who sprang a second later.

When the dust settled we saw the two lions sitting under a tree and noticed that one of them was very old and thin. We thought it possible that he was dependent for hunting on his companion who was in his prime.

In this area a mass of crotalaria marked the course of the river-beds with a golden line. At one point we saw five elephants standing up to their bellies in the yellow sea.

That evening when we returned to the ravine we found the cubs looking very tired. Jespah was particularly lethargic and rested near my car, and whenever Little Elsa came by he licked her and later joined her when she went a little distance away and embraced her. Gopa was already at the meat but it was only after Little Elsa plucked up courage and started on her supper that Jespah came for his cod-liver oil. After this he spent the night close to my car.

Next morning we decided to explore the forty-mile valley in which was the cubs' ravine. For a while we were able to follow a car track, then it faded out and we were obliged to plough our way through shoulder-high grass and whistling thorns. The name sounds attractive, but what it denotes is a scrubby species of acacia which bears double-forked thorns two inches long, and hard, dark-brown galls the size of a golf ball. These are made and inhabited by ants, which defend their homes fiercely when one has the bad luck to brush against them. If the survival of plants in Africa depends on the number of thorns they bear the whistling thorn should outlast all other shrubs. These thorny acacias attract tsetse fly which appreciate their thick cover, so all in all they made our way among them far from pleasant. The farther we drove the more we were plagued by tsetse.

In the circumstances, we naturally saw very little game; only rhino seemed to favour this spiky wilderness, and how we envied them their pachydermatousness.

The valley ended in a wide open plain in which stood a solitary borassus palm, a species which usually grows near water; beside it was a herd of topi, which we estimated to number over three thousand head. We had never before seen so large a herd, though we were later told that in this plain, which is their favourite concentration ground, up to five thousand have been counted.

It had taken us five hours to cover thirty-five miles and we decided to make a detour of eighty-five miles rather than face the ordeal by tsetse, ants and thorns on our return journey, so we drove on to the great plain, where we met many vast herds of game, some of which were using giraffes as sentinels to warn them of the approach of lions, of which we saw several prides.

It was late afternoon when we got back to the cub valley and we were delighted to find the cubs waiting for us. We hoped it might be a sign that they were abandoning their purely nocturnal habits and learning to behave like the lions of the Serengeti, which, assured of their safety, spend their days in the open. If our cubs were able to adapt themselves to a different ecological environment this would not only benefit them, but also make a precedent for moving other doomed lions into new areas with good hope of the success of such releases. It was a cold night and the cubs went off at 10 p.m.

Next day we drove out to get a new kill. On our way we saw a lioness tearing at a freshly killed wildebeeste, while the herd stood within one hundred yards watching her. The lioness paid no attention to them or to us; when on our return some hours later we passed by her she had placed the remains of the carcase near a river-bed and was sleeping in the shade with her four legs in the air, while a short distance away the wildebeeste were peacefully grazing.

When we reached camp we found a letter from the director in which he confirmed in writing that we must leave the Serengeti on the 31st May and added that between now and then we were not permitted to bring any more meat into the camp to feed the cubs.

We drove up to the ravine and found the cubs waiting for us. Jespah was off his feed, did not touch any of the meat and seemed listless. We wondered whether, although it appeared healthy, the open wound round the arrowhead had become infected. Another possibility was that like Elsa at the time of her first release in country very similar to the Serengeti, he had developed an infection due to tsetse fly or ticks and was suffering from fever. He had been listless for a couple of days; now his condition was alarming.

Next morning, feeling anxious about him, we walked along the edge of the cubs' ravine and looked through our field-glasses to see if we could catch sight of him amongst the thick canopy of vegetation. In time we did see the cubs but they spotted us and, alarmed by our presence, rushed towards the cliff. I called to them but they went off. So we set off for home.

The few miles that lay between the cubs' ravine and our camp was the most attractive part of the valley. The river wound its way between small wooded hills in which impala, waterbuck and reedbuck had made their homes. But to-day the peace of the valley was disturbed by the ceaseless barking of large herds of zebra who rushed along as though compelled by some invisible power. The leaders sometimes stopped for a moment, perhaps to investigate the terrain, but soon made up for the pause by pushing ahead at increased speed. At one place the herd was obliged to pass along a narrow space between the river and a steep hill; when they reached this point they packed up densely and nearly piled on top of one another. Having seen this sight I could easily believe a story told me by the park warden. Once he had seen five thousand wildebeeste reach a narrow drinking place; in their frenzy to reach the water the animals climbed on top of one another and when they had gone he found nineteen trampled to death. Our zebras were only a group which had broken off from the main body which numbered some twenty-five thousand head. On our way home we walked up the hill which separated the main valley from the cubs' ravine and from there we could see the mass of zebras, surrounded by about two hundred buffaloes looking like black islands in the striped sea. The whole column was moving quickly.

As we picked our way across the black rocks it struck me that one of these smooth slabs would make a perfect tombstone for Elsa's grave, and I thought it fitting that her stone should come from the cub's new home. To test its durability I scratched a slab with a piece of quartz but could hardly make any impression. Later when a stone-mason engraved Elsa's name on one of these slabs he broke five chisels and told us that neither granite nor marble was so hard and that he would never work again on such a rock.

Next evening the cubs only appeared after dark. This was

disappointing as it showed that they were not yet prepared to abandon their nocturnal habits.

After one lap of cod-liver oil Jespah retired behind the car; when the other cubs had eaten they went over to him and tried to make him play with them, but, though he licked them, he wouldn't move.

At dawn Gopa and Little Elsa had another meal and then went over to Jespah and tried to prod him into going to the ravine with them. After a time he rose slowly and began to follow them. I called and he returned and stood in front of me. I pointed to the meat and talked to him, as I did when I wanted Elsa to eat, and he reacted as his mother used to— went over to the kill and began his meal. It was the first time in three days that we had seen him eat.

Each time Gopa and Little Elsa called to him, he looked up and only started eating again when I said: 'Come on, Jespah, Nyama (meat). Nyama, eat a little more.'

Eventually Gopa came back, and jumping on to Jespah's rump persuaded him to go to the ravine with the others.

During the day we saw a secretary bird that was scratching the ground furiously, whilst obviously taking care to avoid the object he was attacking. Fascinated we watched the stately bird dancing madly on his spindly legs, his quills whipping and flailing with every movement of his head. Spreading his powerful wings he hopped and pecked until finally he tossed a limp snake into the air.

Soon afterwards we noticed two decorative crowned cranes searching the shallows of a swamp for food. This must have been their territory for we were often again to see them there; to-day they were sharing it with a saddle-bill stork, one of the largest birds of the species and certainly the most ornamental, with his vivid red beak crossed by a band of black and his fine black and white plumage.

Having found I still had some terramycin I decided to start treating Jespah with it that evening. It was lucky that only he was prepared to take his cod-liver oil from the dish I held out for him in my hand. Otherwise, no doubt Gopa would have got most of it.

The remains of the carcase were already very high and the cubs, accustomed to fresh meat, sniffed at it with expressions of disgust.

The widespread belief that lions purposefully leave meat in order to allow it to become putrid before eating it is erroneous, though of course when desperately hungry they will eat anything. I could only hope that our cubs would soon learn the art of providing themselves with fresh food; and as I was thinking this Little Elsa walked off determinedly and looked as though she might be going off to search for a kill. Gopa followed her, but Jespah lay still, only occasionally raising his head. When his brother and sister returned he played with them as best he could but it was only too evident that he was ill.

It was unthinkable that we should leave him in this state. So we sent Ibrahim to Seronera with a letter to the park warden explaining the situation and asking for a few days' extension of our permit to stay in the Serengeti. Meanwhile we had no food to give him. So, as we were very short of time, George took it upon himself to drive forty miles outside the boundary of the park to shoot a kill. We realised that this was contrary to our instructions but we hoped that in the circumstances we might be forgiven. Near the border we noticed a low flying aircraft which was we imagined, carrying out a migration census. On our return to camp the park warden who had been a passenger in the plane and had seen George's kill met us and asked us to explain why we had shot an animal in defiance of the prohibition. We apologised, told him of the circumstances and begged him to extend our permit to camp near the cubs. He said that he was not in a position to grant the extension and advised us to get an interview with the director at Arusha. This meant either a two hundred and fifty mile journey by road or chartering an aircraft. Since there was so little time left I chose to go by air, leaving George to look after the cubs. The warden kindly offered to hire a plane for me by radio from Nairobi. It was to collect me next morning. That night we spent as usual with the cubs.

When I left at dawn, Jespah was still in the same listless

state. Ibrahim drove me to Seronera where the plane was to land. When I got there I found that I had left behind at the camp the dress into which I had meant to change. There was no time to go back and collect it; my khaki kit was dirty and I was not very happy at the idea of travelling in this state. However the warden kindly came to my rescue and lent me a shirt and a pair of his shorts in which I set off.

First we flew over the Serengeti Plain; it is richly veined with watercourses and dotted over with bush, in which the stragglers of the migration had gathered. Soon the fertile green changed into deep red soil and next we saw rocky mountain ridges, deep crevasses and cliffs. In the midst of this stony desert lay the nearly dry, gleaming expanse of Lake Natron, its saline deposits, among which flamingos made strange patterns, glistening in the sun.

Above the eerie salt lake the volcano L'ngai (called by the Masai the Mountain of God) towered, looking like a pointed sugar-loaf. We were lucky that no clouds hid the cauldron inside its double crater and we had a good view of the sulphurous fumes which rose from it. Later we flew over several other great craters, including one which contained a lake. The pilot made a detour to show me this and I was most grateful, for it was one of the most beautiful sights I have ever seen. Perpendicular walls framed an absolutely circular piece of bright emerald water, the shores of which were lined by flamingos. Eventually we approached the narrow richly wooded massive ridge of Mondul, the last extinct volcano on our route, and a few moments later were circling above the farms that lie outside Arusha.

Surrounded by their neat coffee plantations, with the roads leading to them bordered by mauve-blossomed jacaranda trees, the farmhouses looked as though they belonged to some collection of nursery toys.

I had been invited to lunch with the director. He was displeased at George's shooting of the last kill against his orders. I apologised and explained our predicament. He then suggested that if we were not happy about the situation, we might recapture the cubs and move them to one of two game reserves in Tanganyika where we would not be subject to the regulations of the national parks and could stay with the lions if they were ill. I was not anxious to move the cubs a second time and after we had looked at a map I was convinced that on other grounds as well the plan was not advisable: both the suggested areas were very narrow and I realised that the cubs might easily cross the protecting boundary and enter thickly populated country. After I had rejected this proposal the director agreed to extend our permit to enable us to stay eight more days with the cubs and to allow us to make three more kills outside the Serengeti between now and the 8th June when we had to leave. To avoid any misunderstanding he put this in writing and left it to us to decide whether to remove the cubs from the Serengeti or after the 8th of June let nature take its course. He also offered to arrange for a meeting between ourselves and the chairman of the trustees if we wanted to put our case before them and ask for more help than he himself could give us.

I arrived back at the camp in a heavy rainstorm feeling depressed and rather ill. All the same, I went up at once to the ravine to join George but no cubs appeared that night and all we heard was the barking of zebra. Next morning I had a high temperature. In spite of this we searched for the cubs in the morning but found no trace of them.

In the evening we returned to the ravine and George was hoisting some meat up a tree when we were startled by a piercing screech coming from inside a hole in the trunk of a tree. Investigating the narrow slit George was surprised to find a young hornbill inside it. The nest was only a foot and a half above ground level where any snake or small predator could easily have got at the young bird.

The cubs arrived soon after dark and made straight for the cod-liver oil. Lately they had become so greedy for it that we had been obliged to ration them, in order not to over-feed them.

When I held out the dish which contained meat mixed with terramycin to Jespah he lifted his paw to push it nearer to the ground, then stopped and kept his paw suspended in the air while he ate up the meat. I wondered whether he had sensed my fear that if his sharp claws touched my hand I should get scratched.

Later a faint lion call attracted the cubs' attention and they went off in the direction it came from.

During their absence we were kept busy chasing hyenas away from the carcase; but they only left when the cubs returned. They quickly ate some more of the meat and then retired into the ravine. As soon as they had gone the hyenas came back and stayed till we hoisted the kill out of their reach. On the following night the lion called again, and the cubs who had hardly touched their dinner went off in his direction. On the third evening Gopa and Little Elsa were very hungry and ate ravenously, but Jespah didn't eat. His condition, thanks no doubt to the terramycin, had improved but he was still far from well, so we decided to take advantage of the director's offer to put our problem to the chairman and beg for a further reprieve. Leaving George in charge of the cubs, I drove one hundred and twenty miles to his farm and had lunch with him.

He believed that the cubs should from now onwards be allowed to face the benefits and hazards of wild life. I suggested that while we were prepared to respect the policy of all national parks, which is to let nature take its course, I knew of many instances in which wardens of the East African Parks had helped ill or starving lions through a critical period, and pointed out that this was in fact an interference with the natural course of events. I stressed that Jespah had received his arrow wound because since early cubhood he had been deprived of a natural life and that we therefore felt responsible for helping to cure his injury. This might entail operating on the wound and in addition he needed our help because of his present low state.

I assured the chairman of our gratitude for the generous hospitality which the trustees had offered the cubs and pointed out how anxious we were that the release should be a complete success. This was unlikely to be the case if we abandoned the cubs before they were old enough to have become competent hunters. However, my arguments did not cause him to alter his point of view or change the date for our final departure.

On my way home I was obliged to camp the night and as I considered our problem it suddenly occurred to me that no one could prevent me from staying on in the Serengeti as a tourist provided I submitted to all park regulations. George would have to return to Isiolo until the government of Kenya had appointed a successor to his job but I could stay on and drive out daily to the ravine to keep an eye on the cubs. True, I would have to camp at one of the official sites near Seronera, which would mean a double journey of fifty miles daily, I would not be allowed to be out at night and there would be no question of feeding the cubs. Still, I would be able to see how they were getting on and this seemed to be the best I could hope for.

It was already the 5th June, and as we had only three days left I thought it best to drive straight to Seronera and book a camping site. As a rule tourists book through a clerk on the staff of Arusha H.Q. I was therefore surprised when I was told that my request to stay as a tourist would need to be submitted to the director and would further require the approval of the chairman. Hoping for the best I put in my application and returned to camp.

Eager to make the most of the few days that remained, we drove to the ravine but the cubs didn't appear till the evening. While we were waiting we watched a solitary impala ram which we had noticed on each of our visits to the glen. He never joined a herd of impala and took no notice of the cubs who for their part never attempted to stalk him. We were astonished at this truce which as it turned out was to last for all the time we spent in the Serengeti.

When Jespah arrived he took his medicine, Gopa rushed at the meat and Little Elsa went off after some zebra which were barking in the distance. It always surprised me that, after dark, animals as vulnerable as zebra should invite trouble by announcing their presence to every predator in the neighbourhood by their barking, but they seemed to have no sense of prudence. This evening the noise went on until Jespah and Gopa joined their sister; then there was a thundering of hooves and the herd departed. Little Elsa came back very hungry and cuffed Jespah when he tried to share the meal, so he went away good-naturedly and sat a little way off till she had finished; then he took the bones in his paws, and rolling his head from side to side scraped a meagre meal from them. He was generous and unselfish as Elsa used to be.

On my drive back to camp next morning some fifty buffalo suddenly emerged from the woods on their way to the river and crossed the track just in front of me. The bull, who kept the rear, came alarmingly close to my car; twice he circled within a few yards of it while I tried to keep my camera steady. Then George's Land-Rover arrived and the bull cantered after the herd. After breakfast George went to get the last kill we were allowed to shoot for the cubs.

On our way home to the cubs' ravine in the late afternoon, we almost ran into a solitary buffalo which was completely absorbed in scratching himself against a thorn-bush; he repeatedly rubbed his massive head at every angle against the branches, no doubt trying to rid himself of parasites, apparently unaware of our presence. Eventually we were obliged to interfere with his grooming for we wanted to reach the cubs' valley before dark. We shouted at him till finally he lifted his huge head and sniffed in our direction, but he was very reluctant to remove himself from our path; at last he slowly retreated looking back at us frequently.

When we came to the ravine and produced the kill the cubs pounced on it. I hated to think that from now on they would have to go through a period of starvation before they had grown into competent hunters. At least Gopa and Little Elsa were in good condition but I felt very concerned about Jespah.

When it started to rain the cubs disappeared and George hoisted the kill, but they had not gone far. When they saw what was happening they rushed back to the meat and hung on to it till we feared the rope would break. When George lowered it they rushed to it and seized the carcase by the throat, trying to suffocate the animal as though it had been a live beast. This was reassuring for it showed that they knew at least the first rule of killing.

On the 7th June I went to Seronera to find out whether I was to be allowed to join the ranks of the tourists. On my road I nearly ran into a lioness who stepped out from behind a bush on to the track. She crossed over determinedly and was soon followed by two tiny cubs. When they joined their mother she licked them affectionately and called to them in low moans just as Elsa used to do to her cubs. Then the little ones trotted off in line behind their mother and disappeared into the long grass.

When I arrived I learned that so long as I behaved as an ordinary visitor I could stay on. I made my way back to camp with a much lighter heart, but was delayed by a pack of six wild dogs; in the N.F.D. these are the most elusive of animals, whose presence is usually only to be observed by the absence of small game. I have never before seen a pack in the open and had not realised what handsome animals they are. Their name is rather misleading as not even a long-legged dog is so slender nor has any dog such big round ears; also wild dogs have only four toes, and are a separate genus. Their colour varies but is always made up of untidy patches of black, white and pale brown in patterns which differ with each individual dog, but each has a fine bushy tail usually with a pure white tip. Wild dogs are probably the most cruel and ruthless of predators; in the chase one dog replaces another till its victim collapses from exhaustion and is torn to pieces. Yet now as they lay in the shade of a tree scrutinising me I was tempted to rank them among the most attractive of wild animals. Obviously the dogs' bellies must have been full, for antelope grazed close to them without either showing any interest in the other. I should never have seen such a sight in the N.F.D. in whose semi-desert country game is less plentiful and the struggle for survival harder, but in the Serengeti, where food is plentiful and the game is protected from interference by men, the wild dogs had evidently developed dif-

ferent habits. I had already observed that this was the case
with lions.

When I came nearer to the camp I saw the dark-maned lion
again; he was accompanied by his mate and another lioness
who had two cubs; they looked about five weeks old. She
was the lioness I had met in the morning and I felt sure that
this was the pride which had chased our cubs from the release
point some weeks ago. The lion allowed the cubs to crawl over
him, but was much more interested in the activities of the
other lioness who was stalking a small herd of zebra. Crouching close to the ground she advanced until she was within
twenty yards of them, but the zebras seemed to feel that so
long as they could see the lioness they were in control of the
situation and showed no signs of alarm. Suddenly a Thomson's
gazelle pranced forward daringly between the zebras and the
lioness and paraded up and down apparently intent on teasing
her. I expected to see the cheeky Tommy pay for his impertinence but nothing happened and when the zebras slowly
moved off the Tommy followed them. Meanwhile the lion
watched the proceedings, giving an occasional low grunt. Then
he moved round an anthill to join his other mate and the two
cubs. They played so charmingly together that I went back to
camp to fetch George and we both returned to spend some
hours watching them. Late in the afternoon heavy clouds
announced a storm and we raced for home.

We had just time to park the cars near the ravine when a
deluge broke upon us. Shivering with cold we remained inside
them while George managed to heat some Ideal milk on a
Primus stove. It poured for many hours. The noise was so
loud that it drowned our calls to the cubs and even when the
rain stopped they failed to put in an appearance.

This was the last night which we would be allowed to spend
in the open and, given the cubs' nocturnal habits, it might well
be the last chance we should have of seeing them. It was therefore with great sadness that I heard the sleepy twitter of
awakening birds and saw dawn break.

A flock of starlings were making their breakfast off the kill and went for George when he began to lower the carcase. We broke up the larger bones and scraped the marrow of which the cubs were so fond, then we dragged all the meat into the ravine and covered it with branches, hoping that no hyena would discover it before the cubs arrived. Then we searched for them; slowly we went along the ravine calling all the familiar names, but saw no sign of the cubs.

While we were packing up I scanned the surroundings through my field-glasses and saw two bateleur eagles soaring high up in the sky. I had noticed them some days earlier gliding through the air, hardly ever changing the perfect curve of their wings. Evidently their territory lay above the cubs' ravine.

George had already started up the engine of his car when on top of the escarpment I noticed a yellow speck which I soon recognised as Jespah's head. I called and in response Gopa and Little Elsa showed up. We couldn't go away without saying good-bye to the cubs, so George switched off his engine and we climbed the escarpment.

Gopa and Little Elsa, unused to being followed into their fortress, bolted for the cover of the ravine, but Jespah sat calmly waiting for us and allowed us to take some photographs of him. Then he slowly went off to join the others, stopping several times to look back at us. Should we ever see the cubs again?

Chapter Sixteen

I BECOME A TOURIST IN THE SERENGETI

IT TOOK most of the day to pack up the camp and it was after tea-time before we reached Seronera. George had to be over the border before dark, so he left in a hurry, taking Ibrahim, Makedde and the cook with him and leaving Nuru and the toto with me.

While Arusha is the main headquarters of the national parks it stands outside the Serengeti. Seronera, as I have said, is the H.Q. within the park. Here the three wardens and their families live and at the lodge tourists can stay; if they want to they can camp in an authorised area about a mile away. I preferred to live in the open, and watch the dawn from my bed in the tent.

So when George had gone we began to pitch camp and then discovered that the poles for the larger tent had been packed up with the things that had gone to Isiolo. All we had left was my little sleeping tent, which was too small to hold all our kit, and the boys' tents.

We were improvising a shelter for our provisions when a cloudburst soaked most of our possessions. During the night several hyenas prowled around and a lion came so close to my tent that I could hear his breathing; luckily the boys were sleeping in the lorry so I did not have to worry about their safety.

Next morning we improved our camp. I had chosen a site on the top of a ridge within the area officially allotted for camping sites. Here, even if the rains were heavy we could be sure of not being bogged down and besides the view was superb. Seronera was a mile and a half away and beyond its small, neat settlement the wooded plain stretched out till on

the east there arose the faint outline of the Ngorongoro crater
and to the west a mountain range near the Uganda border.

Close to the camp two rivulets, at the moment very low, ran
down each side of the ridge. Not far from them were rocky
kopjes with enough shrubby cover to make ideal lairs for lions;
the nearest was three hundred yards from us.

Later in the day I went to Seronera to make arrangements
for my stay and found that I had to hand in our fire-arms as
it was against the regulations for visitors to keep them.

When I asked the warden what I should do if lions visited
me during the night he grinned and replied : ' Shoo them off!'
And certainly by the time I left the Serengeti I became quite an
expert at the ' shooting off' technique. The H.Q. of the
National Parks at Arusha kindly agreed to arrange for my mail
and for food supplies to reach me and also allowed me to
engage one of the Seronera drivers to drive me out daily until
they could find someone in place of Ibrahim to drive the Bedford. I needed a chauffeur because though I have driven since
I was eighteen I am not mechanically minded, could not deal
with a breakdown, and did not want to risk being stuck while
looking for the cubs.

Early next morning we went off with Nuru to look for the
cubs; it was a twenty-five mile drive over skiddy roads to the
ravine. We found the three of them lying under a large tree.
It was nine o'clock by then and I had never before seen them
in the open at such a late hour; I wondered whether they
might have been awaiting our return. The cubs never tried
to find us but had always waited for us to come and look for
them. This was just what Elsa used to do. Indeed, after her
release she always treated us as visitors to her territory. I
thought that the cubs' present behaviour might show that they
did not feel deserted and were sufficiently settled in their new
environment to feel at home : in fact, that the release had
been a success.

I called to the cubs, but they did not move, and when I got
out of the car they bolted. I followed them in the car until
Gopa and Jespah settled under a tree; by then Little Elsa had

disappeared. Next I went to the ravine to see what had happened to the last kill, but could find no trace of the meat.

After this I returned and seeing the two brothers still under their tree, I showed myself and called to them, but they just sat watching me and didn't stir, so I settled down to write letters. Later Gopa went down to the river and after a while was followed by Jespah moving slowly. Two hours later a zebra thundered past, followed by a herd of impala racing as though in flight. Thinking that the cubs must be chasing them I drove to the place where I had seen Jespah disappear and nearly collided with a young blond-maned lion and farther down the valley I saw a full-grown lioness and later two others; but there was no sign of the cubs.

By this time it was necessary to start back for Seronera if we were to be there before dark. We had trouble with the car and next morning by the time the garage had put it right it was 10 a.m., so I had little hope of finding the cubs in the open at the hour at which we would reach the ravine.

As we were driving along I saw a magnificent rufus-maned lion replete and sleepy at a kill; three jackals were also tucking into it but the lion never so much as flicked an ear. Nor did he pay any attention to two young lions with blond ruffs which were sitting some hundred yards away under a tree.

When we reached the ravine it was deserted except for the lone impala ram.

Thinking that the cause of the cubs' nervousness yesterday might have been due to the presence of a strange driver, I had taken only Nuru with me, but we had no luck and had to start back for Seronera after a blank day. The rufus-maned lion and his party had not moved from the place where we had seen them in the morning; a little farther along the track we saw a spotted hyena with two cubs. The youngsters were rather attractive; they had fluffy fur and snub noses, and looked at us with large soft eyes, which had not yet developed the mean expression characteristic of adult hyenas. I took some photos and finally had to drive off the track in order to pass the family.

On our way to the ravine next morning I noticed a dozen spotted hyenas moving in one direction; farther away I saw a dark mass of animals which seemed to be in a heap. Taking my field-glasses I observed six wild dogs on a kill. When they moved aside for a moment I was able to distinguish a hyena cub struggling to its feet, but a second later the dogs were on it again. I couldn't watch six dogs tear a cub to pieces, and this was obviously one of the two I had admired the night before, so I drove ahead as fast as I could and the dogs retreated. I manœuvred the car between them and the cub until it was able to walk slowly over to the hyena pack. The little hyena had some bleeding scratches on its back but did not seem to be in pain or seriously injured. It stopped often to look back at the dogs. When a second cub advanced towards them I didn't know in what direction to move the car or how to head it off quickly enough to protect both cubs simultaneously, but eventually the adult hyenas took over and kept the youngsters safely in their midst. The dogs then developed another interest and, seeming to play, jumped on their hind legs at each other as they cunningly manœuvred close to a few Tommies. Suddenly four of the hyenas rushed at the dogs which to my surprise, ran away. Certainly hyenas have strong jaws and as a pack can be very dangerous, but I would never have expected wild dogs to abandon a victim whose blood they had already tasted when attacked by an inferior number of hyenas.

Among the animals we met that morning were a herd of fifty head of impala. With their lyre-shaped horns, slender well-proportioned bodies and rich red colouring, they are amongst the most beautiful antelopes. At our approach one bounded away gracefully in long leaps, and soon the whole herd was jumping rhythmically. This time they had an excuse for their movement, but often they leap about just for the fun of it. At this season the herds were composed of both sexes, but during certain months, the females keep apart and the males form bachelor herds. We have counted up to forty old and young rams in a single herd and up to seventy ewes, sometimes guarded by a single male.

That day too we drew a blank with the cubs. The driving

was rough and we went into several ant-bear holes which were hidden by the grass and had to jack the wheels out, so I was glad when we got back to Seronera to find that the new driver had arrived.

This man came from Arusha, Tanganyika's tourist centre, and had driven for many years and been in various parts of the country. I set out with him the next morning. We stopped at a small dam near Seronera to fill the radiator, and found two large lions having a drink. The driver was startled as he had never before seen a lion, nor, so he told me, many other wild animals. This was certainly true for he didn't even recognise a rhino. However, by that evening he had had plenty of opportunity of extending his zoological knowledge and was quite blasé when we again passed the pair of lions by the river.

During the day we watched a charming pride consisting of a lioness and two cubs about a year old. They were resting on an ant-hill close to the track. The male cub had a short blond ruff and like Jespah was obviously the protector of the family, for even when his mother and sister retired into the shade he kept guard over them, panting in the sun and never taking his eyes off us for a second. Though we searched everywhere and saw a number of lions, and a few roan antelope which are rare in the Serengeti, we found no trace of the cubs. The new driver was very scared when we met a herd of one hundred buffalo by the river; the steering-wheel wobbled alarmingly and we lost a shock absorber bumping against a rock. From this incident he earned the nickname of John Mbogo (John Buffalo) by which he was known thereafter.

Next morning we met the lioness and the two cubs, which we had seen on the ant-hill, close to the river by the cubs' ravine; they must have walked at least fourteen miles during the twenty-four hours since we had last seen them. Later on I repeatedly met this family between these two points and I could only think that they went all this way to get a drink.

At the entrance to the cubs' valley I recognised the two pairs of mating lions that I had seen there before and when I arrived at the ravine I found the jaw bone of an impala which had recently been killed. I looked round anxiously for the solitary ram and was glad to see him watering a short distance away. I called to the cubs but saw nothing but a hyena sneaking off.

Later we drove a couple of miles to a rivulet which falls from the escarpment and runs across the valley to join the river. Here we found ourselves in lovely parkland, where enormous fig trees grew close to picturesque umbrella acacias, each of which had become the home of many birds, small mammals, lizards and insects. The shade beneath these acacias was so deep that the grass grew shoulder-high and provided ideal lie-ups for all kinds of animals. Even lion and buffalo, lying down in it, were hidden, and one day while we were eating lunch under a tree we were startled to see a dark-maned lion get up from the grass only a few yards from us.

Early morning we left early for the cub valley. The sun was still low and the plains were a sea of sparkling dew from which a mist arose. Wherever we looked we saw animals sleek or fluffy, striped, spotted or plain; with horns and bodies of infinite variety, all leaping and gambolling with a gaiety which was most infectious. Many were conservative in their habits and we got to know a number of individuals quite well.

This morning we spent some time observing the three lions which resembled ours so much that Nuru could not be persuaded that they were not Jespah, Gopa and Little Elsa. To prove to him that he was wrong I called to them but got no response and finally I put a dish of water near the car to test them. When he saw it the leader of the two male cubs growled at me and moved off. It was odd that three cubs about the same age as Elsa's should also have lost their mother, odd too that the lioness not only looked like Elsa but behaved much as she did, though she did not, when sitting, tuck her head between her shoulders as Little Elsa did, and neither of the male cubs had an arrow wound like Jespah or a pot-belly like Gopa. After watching them for several hours I was pretty certain they were a strange pride, yet after we had driven away I began to have doubts, so we returned to have another look at them which confirmed my certainty that they were not our cubs.

Since I was fairly sure that Jespah, Gopa and Little Elsa would not quickly adapt themselves to the tsetse fly or to the proximity of a lot of lions, I searched for them along the base of the escarpment and in ravines farther down the valley where there were no tsetse and fewer lions. One deeply eroded lugga looked particularly promising, for protected by its steep walls I thought the cubs would feel that they could go more safely to the river than by crossing the valley to reach it. There were so many impala near this lugga that we called it the impala lugga. At its far end by the river a pride of lions had their territory. The first time we met them was during the hot hours of the day. We saw a lioness and two almost fully grown female cubs asleep. Nearby was a kill, which though replete they were guarding. A tree above the kill was thick with vultures, and on one of its branches a third female cub sprawled. After a while she stretched herself, yawned, climbed slowly to the ground and flung herself against her mother.

It was very hot and all the lions were panting. Suddenly two of the cubs moved over to a small, bushy tree and climbed on to its slender branches, which shook alarmingly under their weight, but undeterred the lionesses remained aloft, no doubt enjoying the breeze.

On another occasion we came across the same four lionesses making their way to a stagnant pool in the river-bed. The mother walked ahead, at each step cautiously testing the mud with one paw. When she could go no farther without the risk of getting stuck, she consoled herself for not being able to reach the water and drink by looking about for a place to her liking and then resting on the cool mud. Two of the cubs followed her example. We had often seen Elsa acting with the same caution. Lions are always very careful to avoid getting caught in the mud and I cannot recall a case of a lion getting fatally trapped.

This is unfortunately not the case with elephant which during droughts, when crazy with thirst, often become bogged; the harder they struggle to get out the deeper they sink into the sucking mud. We have often tried to rescue elephant from this horrible lingering death. Sometimes several get trapped in the same place. It is possible that a disaster of the kind involving a number of elephant has given rise to the myth of 'elephant cemeteries.' Hippo, rhino and buffalo, on the other hand, all heavy animals which enjoy wallowing in the mud, never seem to get stuck and appear to know by instinct which places are safe for mud bathing and which should be avoided.

A few days later we again met the four lionesses in the same area and also a very large lion. I thought we had better pursue our search farther down the valley, since it was unlikely that our cubs would stay in the territory established by such a pride. We drove the forty miles to the end of the valley where we saw a vast congregation of wildebeeste and zebra; they were plagued by swarms of tsetse, which made me think that this also was a place that the cubs would not choose as their home. The only area we had not so far searched was that of the hills on the far side of the river opposite the cubs' ravine and the hinterland of the escarpment.

The hills were a hopeless proposition since there was no way of driving up them, but I hoped we could reach the edge of the escarpment by making a long detour into the hinterland and reaching the gentler slopes which led up the back of it. To do this, we spent several days bumping over very rough country. John Mbogo was a careful driver but he couldn't avoid hitting rocks or falling into holes that were covered by long grass, and one day we even ground the differential against a buffalo's skull hidden in the grass, the horns of which stuck into the engine. We frequently hit concealed tree-trunks, and while John Mbogo was able to hang on to the steering wheel I would bang my head against the roof and get severely bruised. So eventually I decided to give up the attempt to reach the escarpment; for one thing, I could not afford to have a breakdown in this remote area.

Each day we started out full of hope and each evening returned defeated.

On our homeward journey the sun was behind us and we could watch the animals in a perfect light. The sunsets were superb, the hills turned indigo, the plain straw-coloured. It

Mating lions

A blond maned lion not far from the cub's valley

Zebra; just a few taking part in the vast migration

Wildebeest

Jespah and Gopa wait in a tree above the release point to be fed

Gopa, not yet recovered from the effect of the journey

A pride claims right of way

A leopard . . .

. . . and its larder

Joy and Jespah a few days before the cubs finally disappeared

was dotted with dark brown ant-hills, on which cheetahs and topi often stood out against the sky, and now and then a lion's fluffy mane would rise above the grass as he lifted his head to prospect for his dinner among the grazing herds, while nearby ostriches fanned themselves with their wings and greater bustards strutted about pompously, showing off before the small guinea-fowl and francolins.

Among all the multitude of wild beasts I kept a very soft spot for the bat-eared foxes. Although they are very timid nocturnal animals, we often saw them in the late afternoon, their intelligent eyes peeping out at us from their masklike faces. Their round ears are enormous and I was told by Donald Ker th..t they press them to the ground and listen to discover whether a rat or a mouse, their usual food, is in the offing.

The evening scene appeared very peaceful, yet I knew it was the pause before each predator set out to kill and fill his belly, and there were plenty of hyenas prowling about to remind one of the fact. Unlike the cats which make a straight kill, hyenas either try to benefit by the kill of other predators or make for a newly born antelope calf or some other victim which is unable to defend itself. One day I saw a hyena proudly carrying off the body of a newly born Tommy. Another hyena was hobbling behind him; at intervals the killer shook the carcase provokingly, uttered a high-pitched shriek, stopped, allowed his companion to catch up with him and then went ahead, to repeat his hideous performance.

My nights in camp were often exciting. I could hear lions prowling round and got to recognise the voices of most of them. Once I awoke to hear lapping noises and, being half asleep, listened for some time before I realised that a lioness was inside my tent drinking out of my basin. I had nothing but a table between me and Africa so I shouted at her and urged her to go away which obligingly she did. This incident I reported to the park warden who told me that the lions of the Serengeti were known occasionally to go into tents, pluck at a ground sheet and take a look round to see what was going on.

On another occasion I was kept awake by the snorting of

F.F.   F buffalo and in the light of my torch saw three huge beasts standing within twenty yards of my tent. All I could do was to try to blind them with my light, but they took a long time to make up their minds and I nearly got cramp, holding the torch, before they went off. Hyenas were, of course, always around. I often heard them clattering in the kitchen and they stole several of our cooking pots and other things.

Although some of my nocturnal visitors made my heart beat fast, the roaring of the lions in the stillness of the night never seemed to me a ' blood-curdling noise,' but a most wonderful sound and often appealingly gentle. The lions close to Seronera, having been used to visitors since cubhood, were particularly friendly. Many had been surrounded by cars while suckling their mothers and therefore had come to regard human beings and motors as a natural feature in their lives.

Except in areas in which people have hunted or shot from cars, the wild animals seemed to consider cars as some kind of fellow-creature with strange habits and a peculiar scent, but nevertheless harmless. So long as passengers do not talk too much or move, they too, if they remain inside, do not cause alarm, but when they get out, the animals panic and race away.

Every day we met many lions—but there was never any trace of our cubs. About this time the director paid a short visit to Seronera. I asked him if I might be allowed to spend a few nights inside my car, near to where I thought the cubs would be. I explained that it seemed hopeless to look for them by daylight but that they would probably be attracted by my headlights. He did not, however, feel able to grant me this permission so I carried on as before.

We now searched as close as we could to the hills on the far side of the river. Here we met herds of up to three hundred head of buffalo, and the ground became so rough that we became frequent customers at the Seronera repair workshops. The warden in charge of it was always cheerful and ready to work on the car at all hours and I was most grateful to him.

The dry season had come and the animals were now dependent on water holes and such rivers as did not dry up.

This was the time of year when poachers' activities were at their height. Since they knew exactly where the animals must pass to quench their thirst, the wardens worked very hard to counteract their activities and it was horrifying to see the number of snares, poisoned arrows and spears which they confiscated and to realise how small a proportion of the total of weapons and traps these represented: wire for snares is cheap and can be bought from any Indian trader.

The most effective method of trapping is to pile up cut thorn bushes in a long line close to a water hole, leaving occasional gaps in which snares are set. A noose held in shape by strong grass is fastened to twigs at the level of the animal's head and a heavy log is attached to the end of the wire. The struggle of an animal caught in the snare automatically tightens the noose, then either it strangles itself or dies a lingering death as the wire victims may be eaten by hyenas.

At the peak of the season poachers have set so many snares they don't even bother to collect all their prey. In flimsy wooden shelters made out of local shrub they cut the meat into thin strips, hang it up to dry and then sell it as biltong. But many animals are killed only for their tails which are sold as fly switches at thirty shillings each, and the waste of meat and skins is unbelievable. Snaring is popular because it involves no danger or physical effort, whereas killing by poisoned arrows requires the hunter to be on the spot, though often this way of killing is used only to finish off a snared animal. Alternatively, a poacher may sit up in a tree near to a water hole or by a well-used game path. Then when an animal passes below he shoots his arrow. If the poison is fresh, it is so deadly that even a superficial scratch will cause death within a few minutes. It is obtained very easily from Acocanthera Friesiorum, a small tree which grows at an altitude of five thousand to six thousand feet in many parts of East Africa.

The Africans make a decoction of its leaves, twigs and bark and smear the thick pitch-like substance upon arrowheads. When this has dried they wrap the arrowhead in fibre, which they only remove immediately before use. Besides these home-made weapons poachers use important gin traps, muzzle-loader rifles and shot-guns. Apart from individual poaching there are well organised parties, supplied with motorised transport and financed by traders.

To give an idea of the scale of the poaching I will quote a few illustrative paragraphs from some of the monthly reports on poaching activities along the boundary of the Serengeti :

May . . . intense motorised poaching has already started both inside and outside the park. At least six lorries and Land-Rovers are working on the lower Rowana and the Mwama-deo area near Handagego operating in a shuttle service to the Ikizu butchers and at times carrying two loads of meat a day.

June . . . with the return of our migrating herds from the central plains there was a serious increase in poaching. Mr. Whalley, Game Ranger Mwanza, did a splendid job collecting over two hundred wire snares and destroying five big poacher gangs. At Nyamuma . . . park guards caught one Wasukuma with no less than fifty-four wildebeeste tails, the result of six days' bow and poisoned arrow hunting.

The July report notes among other activities five big camps destroyed in the western corridor and the arrest of Wakuria dealers in arrow poison, the amount of poison confiscated being enough to equip two thousand arrows, the destruction of two hundred steel snares in one area of fifty in another, and the arrest of seventy-three poachers. Last year one hundred and eighty-five poachers were convicted and over a period of six years ten thousand wire snares were confiscated.

Amongst horrible incidents were : a buffalo that must have been caught in a snare dying by inches for several weeks, and a hen ostrich dead in a snare on her nest which contained nineteen eggs.

The staff of the Serengeti do all that is humanly possible to put down poaching, often in very dangerous circumstances. The July report for 1959 mentions one incident in which a poacher tried to strangle one of the porters, another in which a poisoned arrow was shot at a guard and a third in which an attempt was made to stab a guard with a handful of poisoned arrows.

All over East Africa poaching, drought, floods and the legal destruction of wild animals to make place for men and their crops, threaten the survival of wild life. The idea that they may one day become extinct appals me. The longer I live among animals the more I want to help them and the more I believe that in helping them we also help man, for if we exterminate all the wild animals we shall upset the balance of creation of which we ourselves are a part. A Quaker paper has made a very apposite remark on our relationship to animals, saying approximately that we are apt to overlook the fact that when in the beginning man was said to have been given dominion over the animals he was without sin, for he had not then disobeyed God, and he lived in daily communion with him.[1]

Since to-day we no longer live in the Garden of Eden what are the practical steps we can take to make sure of the conservation of wild life? First, we have to face the fact that the practicability of preserving wild beasts in any given area depends primarily on the degree of pressure of its human population. And this being so, funds are needed to create more game reserves and national parks, to finance and administer these sanctuaries, to support a qualified staff, to combat poaching, and enforce game laws within them, to make bore holes and dams in areas threatened by drought and to equip rescue teams to move doomed animals into these sanctuaries. But even if all these things were provided the schemes would be destined to failure if they lacked wholehearted African support. This in its turn means that funds must be available for educating Africans to be proud of their fauna, which as well as all else is a vital asset to their economy. Extensive ecological research into the type of country in which wild animals live is another necessity. Without these long-term policies the short-term expedients will be wasted, even though without the latter animals would not survive long enough to benefit from long-term plans.

[1] 'Eastward in Eden', *The Friend*, 5th August 1960.

As I drove out daily in search of the cubs, I had plenty of time to think about these problems and to wonder why man should be divorcing himself from natural life; yet the many letters I received about the Elsa books assured me that an immense number of people would in fact like to live a life which kept them in relation with nature and wild animals, and I thought how much they would enjoy seeing, instead of reading about, the lionesses with their cubs which at that moment were blocking our track, stretching out lazily in the sun and not showing any intention of letting us go by (and whose track was it anyway?).

I have always been surprised that lions are so sure of themselves, while the reactions of leopards and cheetahs are so different; this is particularly strange as leopards are considered by many hunters to be more dangerous than lions, and cheetahs can outrun any predator. Nevertheless they always bolted when they saw us, even if they were on a kill. Once I found a leopard's larder consisting of a freshly killed bushbuck wedged high up in a tree and waited for him to return, but he never dared to come near the place while we were there.

The only friendly leopards I ever came across were a pair at Seronera, one of which had cubs; they, it appeared, were so used to being admired by visitors that they had become indifferent to them. One who had earned the nickname 'Good as Gold', owing to his superb gold coat and obliging habits, used to walk alongside my car, roll in front of the bumper and sharpen his claws on a tree-trunk within a few feet of us. At other times, he would stretch himself on a fallen tree-trunk so near to me that I could have touched him, but 'Good as Gold' was a most unusual leopard.

As the days passed in fruitless search, I became more and more depressed and finally wrote to George to come back and help me to find the cubs.

A few days later the director and a park warden visited my camp. I took the opportunity to renew my request to be allowed to spend a few nights out in the car in the hope that the cubs would be attracted by the headlights and I also asked if I might be allowed to walk up the escarpment and in the hills, if necessary escorted by an armed African ranger. I stressed again the condition of Jespah's wound and the youth of the cubs. The director replied that at the trustees' next meeting he would put my requests before them; meanwhile he suggested that I should write to the chairman. This I did.

One evening while I was typing I was startled by hearing an English voice and looking round saw three men. They were farmers from Kenya who were on holiday and they had pitched their tent within a few yards of mine. Seeing my light they had walked across to invite me to have a drink with them.

I was startled that they should have crossed even this short distance without a light, and I pointed out that there were lions about and plenty of cover for them. The men laughed at my anxiety, but accepted my lamp to guide them back.

The next night I dined with them and was astonished to see that they had no tent and slept in the open on camp-beds only five inches off the ground. When I asked them what they would do if a lion called on them while they were sleeping they laughed and obviously regarded me as a nervous woman.

Next morning we met again at the rivulet below the camp site; we had to stop as our path was barred by a pride of thirteen lions, which showed no sign of moving out of our way. Among them were several cubs of varying ages. One young lion, with a friendly expression and a sprouting ruff, reminded me very much of Jespah and I was watching him so intently that I never noticed the approach of his father, until he brushed against the bumper of my car. Eventually the pride moved off and we were able to go on. The farmers left that day and when I returned in the evening I found a bottle of wine and a letter telling me to cheer up and stop worrying about who called in after dark. I hoped they were right but still thought it asking for trouble to sleep in the open on such low camp-beds.

On the 1st of July I paid John Mbogo, in fact I overpaid him by a couple of pounds, and he took the occasion to disappear, so I was left without a driver and was very thankful to receive a telegram from George saying that he would arrive on the 4th July. Meanwhile I drove and Nuru came with me to jack us out of the holes we got stuck in.

On one of these drives we came across the body of a very young buffalo calf; it had no wound except a small hole in its belly and I could only imagine that it must have been killed by a ratel. Ratels are the most fearless animals and quite capable of attacking a baby buffalo from beneath. Close to Seronera I met a safari party who told me of a spot close to the river where I could see a leopard with two cubs, so early next morning I went in search of them. But all I found was the head of one cub. A white hunter who appeared soon afterwards said it had been killed by a lion. For a lion to kill a leopard seems near to cannibalism. But there is certainly an enmity between these two species of cats. I had heard of a leopard cub killed by lions while its mother took refuge in a tree and George had known of several cases in the N.F.D. of leopards killing lion cubs. There are, however, to my knowledge no instances of adult lions and leopards fighting or killing each other.

Now, close to the remains of the leopard cub I saw a blond-maned lion, three lionesses and six cubs, five of whom can have been no more than about six weeks old. They kept close to one lioness and suckled her, while the older cub stayed with the lioness who was no doubt his mother. The third lioness had dry teats and may have been the ' aunt '; she had a nasty gash on her chest, perhaps acquired in hunting for the pride. The lion remained some two hundred yards away from the rest of the family, but did not object to my watching them from very close range. The cubs were intrigued by the car and came right up to it. I stayed observing the pride for a couple of hours, by which time they were all sound asleep. On my way home I was stopped by a safari party who told me that, the night before, a pair of lions had passed within a few yards of their tent and that one of them was limping.

On my return I found George in camp. He had been away nearly a month and had now taken ten days' leave and so anxious was he not to waste a moment of it that he had driven all through the night. His journey had been exciting. At about

1 a.m., when he was climbing up a narrow road through thick forest, with a deep ravine on one side and a steep bank on the other, a rhino had suddenly showed up in his headlights. It was walking down the middle of the road and coming towards him. He pulled his car up close to the right bank as he did not wish to risk being pushed into the ravine. The rhino who had been moving fast came to an abrupt stop in front of the bonnet bumper. After this he tried to squeeze between the bank and the car, but, finding it too tight a fit, backed out and turned round. Perhaps he too didn't want to be pushed into the ravine or maybe he was observing the rule of the road and wished to pass on the correct side. George gave him twenty minutes' start and then drove off but soon found the rhino still plodding along the track and had to wait some time till he turned into the forest.

In spite of a sleepless night George was ready to start off at once in search of the cubs, but first he gave me the director's interim reply to our appeal to the trustees asking permission to sleep out. It only said that the trustees had discussed our letter and that he was writing officially to let us know what they decided. He added that he hoped we would feel that they had not been unsympathetic in the matter. This didn't tell us much but made us hopeful.

Knowing that the park warden had been to Arusha and was expected back that evening I called on him hoping that he might have brought the letter. He had and this is what it said:

They were glad that when we had last seen the cubs they were in good fettle and that we were happy about the release area.

If we agreed to certain conditions they would be glad to grant our requests. George and I could sleep out for not more than seven nights and offer the cubs water and cod-liver oil if they came to us. During this time we were allowed to walk on the escarpment and elsewhere at our own risk and George was permitted to carry fire-arms for self-defence.

The trustees stressed that where the cubs were to continue to live rested entirely with us and that if we thought they had a better chance in some place other than the Serengeti we could decide to move them out of the park. The director added that, as we knew, he had obtained the Tanganyika Game Department's permission to move them into the Mkomazi Game Reserve where conditions were most nearly akin to those prevailing in Elsa's camp, and pointed out that this reserve not being a national park it would presumably be easier for us to stay with them, which was not possible in a national park.

He then listed the conditions to which we must agree.

1. We were to have our cages sent at once to the area in which we were going to search.
2. If and when we found the lions we should then decide whether to move them or not.
3. If we decided not to move them we were to leave the park finally and not expect any more exceptions to the regulations to be granted us.
4. If we decided to move them we should let the park warden know of our decision immediately.
5. We were to make no kill without first getting permission from the park warden.
6. We were to keep the park warden advised about every other day of what was going on.

Finally the trustees sent their good wishes for the success of our search and hoped we should find the cubs fit and well.

I asked the park warden : if we found the cubs emaciated while he happened to be on safari, how could we obtain permission to feed them? He advised me in this event to contact the director by radio and discuss the problem with him.

Driving back I passed a safari party which had just arrived and had pitched their tents a few hundred yards from ours. They were farmers from Kenya.

We then packed our cars for a week's absence. As a result of camping out among wild animals I have become a light sleeper and that night I woke to hear the distant engine of a car. Some moments later the park warden arrived and told us to move at once into the cars as a lion had taken a visitor from a camp near ours and was still prowling around. He asked if we had any morphia with us as there was none in

Seronera. The man had been badly mauled. Luckily George had two ampoules, so we gave the warden these and all our supply of sulphonamide. He told us that there was a charter plane in the area which could take the injured man at first light to Nairobi, then assuring us that there was nothing we could do to help, he left and not long afterwards we heard the plane take off.

Meanwhile George had told Nuru and the rest of our staff to light lamps and keep awake.

Very early we went to the scene of the incident, only three hundred yards from our camp, to find out whether the friends of the unfortunate man needed any help. Our spooring revealed that two lions had come past our camp and gone along the car track leading to the next camp and had stopped abreast of it. The spoor was that of two male lions; one was considerably larger than the other. The bigger lion had gone up to the camp fire, seized a large enamel jug and bitten through it, an indication of the capacity of his jaws. The camping party had consisted of five people, a married couple who had a tent of their own, the entrance flaps of which they had closed for the night, and three men who shared a tent. The night was warm so the men had not put up their mosquito nets and had placed their low camp-beds in a row. They lay with their heads at the entrance of the tent which they left open. One had placed a basin set on a stand behind his head, the man next to him had the middle tent pole as a protection but the third had nothing between him and the world outside. During the night the farmer in the middle bed, woken by a low moaning sound, noticed that his neighbour's bed was empty and disarranged. He switched on a torch and, fifteen yards away, saw a lion with his friend's head in its mouth. He roused the camp, and two African servants very courageously rushed towards the lion; one flung a panga (a long knife) at it. Possibly this hit the lion for he dropped the man, bit viciously at the handle of the panga and moved a short distance away. The injured farmer was quickly rescued. Meanwhile the lion continued to circle the camp and was only kept off by having a car driven towards him.

Among the visitors at the lodge there was a European dresser who was able to attend to the farmer's wounds, and then the park wardens and their wives cared for him until the plane was able to take off and fly him to Nairobi; unfortunately his wounds proved fatal and he died on the operating table.

This was the first fatal accident to take place in the Serengeti since it became a national park. That morning two of the park wardens shot both lions. The larger one was found to have a septic wound in his shoulder, which no doubt was a serious handicap to his hunting activities. In such circumstances any lion in any part of Africa will not hesitate to kill a human being. We felt sure that this injured lion was the limping lion which the safari party had told us about some days ago.

Chapter Seventeen

WE SEE THE CUBS AGAIN

THE DIRECTOR arrived by plane that morning and we had a talk with him. He confirmed the concession to sleep out in the cub valley for seven nights but so far as preparing for feeding the cubs should we find them emaciated, he advised us not to cross our bridges before we came to them, and added that in an emergency the park warden might be able to help us. George had only eight days' leave left so we decided that we would not have time to collect the crates though this was a condition mentioned in the letter. In any case we could not know whether or not they would be needed. Before we could start we had to move our camp to Seronera, as in view of the accident no more camping was to be allowed till security measures had been taken.

As a result it was late in the day before we set off to the cub ravine. When we got there we parked our cars in the middle of the small plain where George had seen the cubs in May. We turned on a light and soon a large young blond-maned lion came to investigate it. He stopped for a few moments, watched us and then walked off towards the second ravine which was not far away.

No cubs showed up during that night.

Early in the morning we drove near to the cubs' ravine and climbed the escarpment above it where nearly a month ago we had seen the cubs. We walked along its crest for nearly three hours, calling repeatedly but in vain. Then we came down into the next valley and walked back to the car. As we reached the top of a rise which led into the cub ravine George grabbed me by the shoulder. There were all three cubs sitting by the cars waiting for us. They behaved in the most matter-of-fact manner as though we had never left them. Jespah came to greet us giving the soft moans with which Elsa always welcomed us. He allowed me to pat his head and then sat and watched us as we went over to the other cubs. They went off as we approached and settled under a tree. But when we offered them cod-liver oil and water they came and lapped it up quickly. They were thin but in fair condition though Jespah and Gopa had now completely lost their ruffs and looked like lionesses. Jespah's coat was no longer shining and he still carried the arrow. The wound was discharging a thin serum which attracted flies and which he licked repeatedly; he also had some small scars probably gained in combat with other animals. He was very friendly and came close to us but would not allow us to pull at the arrowhead.

It was wonderful to see the cubs again and as we watched them we discussed several puzzling questions. Why had the lions lost their ruffs? We knew that under stress domestic cats sometimes moult. Could Jespah and Gopa have become maneless owing to the strain of adapting themselves to a new environment? Why had they turned up to-day? Had they seen the light during the night and realised that we were there? Or had they been hiding when I searched in the cub valley during the last month and been too frightened of John Mbogo and Nuru to come into the open?

Though previously they had always taken cover during the hot hours of the day, now they stayed in the light shade of a tree while we lunched. When George went off to collect the second car which we had left in the plain, this didn't disturb them and for all the rest of that day they remained in the open. In fact they seemed to be adopting the habits of the Serengeti lions.

The solitary impala ram was present all the time. Towards dark he moved in a leisurely way down the hill grazing as he went. Little Elsa stalked him and after a while Jespah followed. So long as the ram was feeding they crouched low and wriggled towards him but when he looked in their direction they froze. Gopa remained behind watching the hunt. Finally, the impala dashed off and the cubs returned.

We had stored some of our kit beside our camp-beds inside the cars and the rest on the roof. Jespah inspected these objects hoping perhaps to find his dinner, and even Gopa and Little Elsa came close to us, but we had nothing for them but cod-liver oil. We allowed them to drink as much of this as we thought good for them, then they settled close to our car and during the night we heard them playing. Jespah visited us several times, no doubt puzzled that we had not given him any meat.

After the weeks of anxiety it was a tremendous relief to know that the release had proved a success and that the cubs were in relatively good condition : the only worry was Jespah's discharging wound and his dull coat. We could not consider moving the cubs again after all they had been through, nor did we want to remove Jespah separately if he could be operated on in the Serengeti. So we decided to use our week to try to get him in better condition and then try to make arrangements to have him operated upon. The days now at our disposal did not allow us time to do this.

Next morning we found the cubs under a bush about four hundred yards down the hill. Jespah came at once and placed himself between us and his brother and sister and I gave him his cod-liver oil. That morning his coat was much worse than it had been when we first saw him and he was covered with swellings the size of peas. This worried us but we did not wish to raise a false alarm about it until we were sure what the swellings were due to; they looked rather similar to swellings which Elsa had sometimes developed after rolling on ants. However, we could not be sure that this was what they were and would have to keep Jespah under observation. This meant feeding the cubs who would otherwise need to go off hunting.

George therefore drove off to Seronera to get permission to feed the cubs and to send a cable to the publishers of the Elsa books to give them our good news.

In his enthusiasm he worded this telegram and also a similar one to the director at Arusha over-optimistically : ' cubs found in excellent condition.' This wording caused a false impression and later gave rise to a grave misunderstanding. While George was away I watched the cubs dozing under a bush.

About lunch-time a herd of some hundred and twenty Tommies appeared together with the impala ram. On seeing me they stopped, turned towards the cubs and began grazing within twenty yards of them. One cheeky Tommy even went up to their bush and indeed the whole herd behaved as though no lions were about. The cubs sat on their haunches, heads on their paws, watching. This went on for half an hour, then, suddenly, Little Elsa rushed full speed at the herd which fled into the valley except for some twenty-five Tommies which got cut off and remained behind. A little later she chased these too, but plainly only for the fun of it. Neither side took the game seriously until Gopa and Jespah joined in the hunt, when the Tommies clattered over the rocks and up the hill, all except one small fawn and its father, which stood quietly watching the proceedings and only left after the cubs had returned. Then they walked slowly down the valley to rejoin the others. Half-way there they were met by the fawn's mother who licked it and guided it safely back to the herd.

George returned without a kill; the park warden had been absent, so he had waited till the afternoon when he could speak to the director over the radio. He obtained permission to buy two goats at a small village outside the park, some sixty miles away, but since he could not get there and back in the day he had to put off getting the goats till the next day.

At dusk the cubs came looking for their dinner but as we had only cod-liver oil to give them they left early. Next morning George drove off to get the goats and I sorted out our kit and aired our bedding. The cubs arrived while everything was still laid out on the ground. This provided them with a splendid game, but they were very good-natured and in the end allowed me to collect all our possessions undamaged. After this they retired into the shade of a bush where they spent the rest of the day.

George arrived at 6 p.m. with the goats. The moment he saw the meat, Jespah seized it and raced away with it; Gopa and Little Elsa chased him and there was a scrimmage. The three cubs sat, noses together, holding on to the carcase, tempers grew hot and there were growls and spittings; for an hour the deadlock went on and not one of them would give way. Then Gopa made a try to go off with the meat, but Jespah grabbed it instantly and another deadlock ensued. With ears flattened and given angry snarls the brothers faced each other while Little Elsa quietly gnawed away. Finally Jespah and Gopa relaxed and the three cubs ate amicably together.

The second carcase we placed on the roof of the car, thinking it would be safe there till to-morrow, as the cubs had never tried to get on to the cars. But early in the morning I was woken by a heavy thud and found the car rocking violently. The next moment I saw Jespah jump with the carcase from the roof on to the bonnet and make off with it to the ravine followed by the other cubs.

A couple of hours later he reappeared and leapt on to the roof of the car where we had stored our surplus kit and found a lot of things there to delight him: cardboard boxes filled with bottles, my plant press, a rubber cushion, a folding armchair. Busily he emptied the boxes, clattering their contents on to the ground. Then he tried to get at the blotting-paper inside the plant press and when defeated threw it overboard. He also ransacked the rest of our kit. When he had finished he rested his head on his paws and blinked at us. His brother and sister had watched him intently but had not ventured to join him; now they went off to play on a fallen tree where Jespah soon joined them. The three cubs prodded each other playfully for a while and then disappeared into the ravine.

We noticed a lot of vultures circling above the crest of the nearest hill and supposed they were leaving a kill, probably one made by the lion which I had heard roaring close by during the night. After lunch we went to look for the cubs and found them asleep in the dense cover at the base of the cliff. Next to them was the carcase of a freshly-killed reedbuck. Whether they had killed it or stolen it off a leopard we couldn't tell. That a kill should have taken place so close to us without our hearing a sound was odd enough.

In the evening we went back to the cubs and found that they had practically finished the reedbuck and had dragged what remains were left into cover. We could hear the lions breathing in the thicket but we could not see them. It seemed extraordinary that such large animals could hide themselves so completely—particularly as we knew to within a few feet where they were. Later the coughing of a leopard told us who had made the kill.

When it was dark the cubs came for a drink and spent the night near us but by morning they had gone off. After lunch they emerged from the ravine and Jespah hopped on to the roof of my car, while Gopa and Little Elsa lay under the shade of a tree some fifty yards away. I wondered why Jespah preferred to get on my car rather than George's. Had he got used to thinking it was *his* car, or did it look to him the more comfortable of the two? Elsa had always preferred George's car.

The impala ram was present as usual; he gave snorts and grunts but the cubs took no notice of him. Little Elsa spent some time stalking Tommies but was evidently not out for a kill and soon settled down. I sat close to Jespah and whenever my position allowed I tried to pull at the arrow. He made no objection to my twiddling the protruding shank, but it was firmly fixed as ever and there was no sign of its sloughing out. The point of the arrow was just below the skin and a small slit might well suffice to pull it out point first. The swellings, probably due to ant bites, had disappeared, but his coat looked dull and shabby. But when the setting sun turned it to gold, his features and his expression were so like his mother's that when he looked at me intently, as she used to do, I suddenly had the impression that Elsa had returned. While he allowed me to pat his paw and stroke his nostrils he shut his eyes and I closed mine. Then I felt certain that Elsa was there. After I opened my eyes again I felt strangely free.

When night came we retired to our cars. Very soon the canvas roof of mine sagged under Jespah's weight and from my bed I was able to pat him through the canvas. Later George was woken by the swaying of his car and found Jespah leaning over the tailboard looking at him as though he wanted

to come in. There was no sign of the others and Jespah himself left at dawn.

We spent the morning looking for the lions and found no
trace of them; but at tea-time they came up from the valley
in which we had been looking for them and Jespah seated
himself on the bonnet of my car. I made a last attempt to
move the arrow but without success.

To-morrow we should have to leave the cubs and we could
have been fairly happy about them had it not been for Jespah's
wound. However little it seemed to encumber him at the
moment, it had obviously weakened his condition and was a
source of infection as his dull coat proved. In combat with a
prey the skin might get torn or the arrowhead packed deeper
and either of these possibilities might cause serious damage
which would ultimately impair his capacity to hunt. In the
circumstances the sooner he could be operated on the better.
We discussed the situation and decided to cut our time with
the cubs short and leave as early as was possible the next morning, so that we could speak over the radio to the director and
get permission to carry out the operation. For this we should
need a crate in which to confine Jespah and a veterinary surgeon to give the anæsthetic and perform the operation. George
was sure his leave would be extended for the time necessary to
make the arrangements and get the operation performed.

When it was dark Jespah came for his cod-liver oil. There
was not much left in the gallon tin we had opened six days
ago and I wanted to divide it equally among the cubs. When
Jespah saw me holding the tin he tried to seize it. I said
'No, Jespah, no,' and looking puzzled and hurt he at once
turned away. After this I poured the oil into three dishes.
Gopa and Little Elsa drank theirs up at once, but Jespah was
offended and would not come near the dish I held out to him.
I dared not put it on the ground for then the others would
have finished it off, so I tried my best to get into favour again.
But Jespah looked stonily in the opposite direction and ignored
me.

We passed the evening watching the cubs licking each other

and rolling about affectionately together behind the cars. They left about 11 p.m. This was the last we were to see of them though at the time we expected to return soon with a vet.

Later in the night we heard some lions calling in a low voice to each other and hoped it might be our cubs hunting.

Next morning we left for Seronera, hoping to arrange facilities to operate on Jespah at once. These were denied. On our way through Arusha we approached the director again. He advised us to appeal to the trustees who were holding their next meeting in August. With a heavy heart we left Tanganyika.

Chapter Eighteen

THE LONG SEARCH

WHEN WE got to Nairobi we heard the good news that Ken Smith could now take over as Senior Warden of the N.F.D., leaving George free to help with the cubs. We wrote to the director of the Tanganyika National Parks, asking him to submit our request for permission to operate on Jespah, to the trustees at their mid-August meeting.

I went first to Isiolo to move our furniture out of the Government house in which we had been living and into one which we had rented from the National Parks of Kenya and which was about eight miles from our old home. Meanwhile, George set off to help to move a herd of Thomas kob which were living in an area where their presence clashed with human interest, to a game reserve, 300 miles away. This operation was being financed partly by the Game Department, partly by the Elsa Appeal and partly by royalties from the Elsa books. These Thomas kob are not only beautiful antelope, but their herd which numbers about 500 head is the only one of the species in Kenya.

Towards the end of August Billy Collins paid another visit to East Africa. He came in the hope of getting a last sight of the cubs and to attend the Arusha Conference. This conference was the first to which people from all over the world, who were interested in the preservation of wild life, had been invited to come together to discuss the conservation of game in East Africa.

Billy Collins's arrival in Nairobi coincided with the receipt of a telegram from the director, informing us that the trustees had refused permission for an operation to be performed on Jespah.

Doctor T. Harthoorn, of Makarere Veterinary College, one

of the most distinguished veterinary surgeons in Africa, had already agreed to do the operation, should Jespah be found in a state which demanded an intervention. As he happened to be in Nairobi at this time we were able to talk over with him, and also with Noel Simon, Founder and Chairman of the East African Wild Life Society, and Major Grimwood what, in view of the new blow to our hopes, we should now do.

We decided that Billy and I should go to the Serengeti and spend a week there trying to find the cubs and that Billy would see the chairman in Arusha and try to persuade him to change his mind, and allow Dr. Harthoorn to operate, if this were possible and if he considered it necessary.

On our way we visited the Amboseli National Park close to the Tanganyika border. Amboseli is a dried-up lake, which lies at the foot of Kilimanjaro; its salt deposits attract a great variety of game.

We arrived there on a beautiful afternoon. The deep red plain, which in the dry season is often swept by sudden whirlwinds and dust storms, was covered with low sage bushes, now turned to gold by the setting sun; in the foreground four elephants stood under a palm-tree while a rhino emerged from a nearby bush. Billy had never till then seen one in the wild; but before he returned to Europe he was to see fourteen taking their evening stroll.

We also watched other game, including a herd of buffalo, which were obviously quite used to the presence of human beings and of cars.

This made me wonder how many tourists who see animals only in national parks go away with the impression that there is no preservation problem and fail to realise that, outside these sanctuaries, wild life is disappearing at an alarming rate.

On our way through Arusha, Billy called on the director and discussed our wish to be allowed to sleep out in order to find the cubs and to have permission to operate on Jespah, if when we found him this seemed necessary. This conversation did not result in any change of attitude on the director's part; but they agreed that after our search for the cubs, Billy should see the chairman and talk the matter over with him.

We then went on to Lake Manyara. Here we watched two ostriches racing about in shallow water. Near them were about twenty buffalo and fifty reedbuck surrounded by flocks of flamingo, marabou stork, Egyptian geese and all sorts of water fowl. Some of the reedbuck were lying partly submerged and the flamingo were searching for food within a few feet of them, but the sight which surprised me was that of the ostriches taking to water. However, when we reached the Flamingo Hotel we learned the cause of their strange behaviour. Apparently, before Lake Manyara became a national park, these birds were molested by people to such an extent that only this pair had survived; and whenever they saw a car approaching they rushed for safety to the water.

Next morning the weather was overcast, so we saw no views. We called on the game warden who lives near the Ngorongoro crater and were introduced to Ngugu, his tame porcupine, a great personality who nuzzled up to anyone who offered him fruit or a piece of cake. We then went on to the lodge at Seronera, where we spent six days.

Early in the morning after our arrival we set off for the cubs' release point. We found it occupied by a party of surveyors who had been living there for the last month. We asked them what lions they had seen. They had seen many, but could not, of course, know whether the cubs had been among them.

Then we went up to the cub ravine and I called Jespah, Gopa, Little Elsa, but there was no response. So we continued up the valley. Every time we saw trees covered with vulture, we drove up to them, hoping to find the cubs on a kill but were always disappointed. We found several pride of lion and at one point came very close to a herd of 200 buffalo and were obliged to drive off very quickly indeed.

We stayed as late as was possible if we were to comply with the regulation that compelled tourists to be back at Seronera before dark.

On our way home we saw a most beautiful cheetah standing on an ant-hill silhouetted against the setting sun. Soon afterwards a leopard crossed our track: it had dense black markings which gave its fur a bluish sheen. After a few moments he glided, rather than ran, out of our sight.

Next day we went again at first light to the cub valley where we found a pair of male lions, one of which had a badly injured eye. The able-bodied lion stayed with his sick friend and I hoped he would hunt for him.

Then we searched along the river where, owing to the drought, there was a bigger concentration of animals than I had ever seen before. Finally we went back to the ravine and called for a long time but saw no sign of the cubs.

On our way home we again saw the beautiful cheetah on his ant-hill and at a big pond a leopard and a saddlebill stork quenching their thirst.

By the fourth day Billy was obviously unwell. He had been unmercifully bitten by tsetse, his arms and legs were very swollen and I was thankful that a doctor happened to be staying at the lodge. He diagnosed an allergy, prescribed remedies and advised Billy not to go back to the tsetse-infected area. Therefore during the last three days of our visit we stayed close to Seronera. It was disappointing not to be able to go on searching for the cubs, but there was plenty of game to watch near the lodge. In the early hours of the morning we saw some bat-eared foxes and later a pride of lion lying in the open close to a kopje. The pride, which was a large one, consisted of three maned lions, three lionesses, six suckling cubs about four weeks old, and two young male lions round about Jespah's age. They were all so sleepy that they paid no attention to us nor to a young cheetah who was basking in the sunshine a hundred yards away.

When it got hot we retired to the shade of a tree near my former camp site and I tried to write, but was distracted by a pair of giraffe with two small calves. Their stumpy horns had not yet hardened and looked like tufts of hair; their necks were absolutely short but they had enormous shoulders and knobbly knees quite out of proportion to the rest of their body.

One evening we dined with the park warden and his wife and met the director who suggested that on the following day we should witness the release of a rhino which had been brought to the park from an area where it interfered with a settlement scheme. It was the first release of this type and the chairman and Peter Scott and other guests who were attending the Arusha Conference were coming to see it.

A great many people arrived to see the release; thirty came by a Sunday excursion plane and there was such a convoy of cars, that by the time everyone had parked their vehicles near the lorry containing the crate I began to wonder how the animal would find its way to freedom. When the doors of the crate were opened and the rhino became visible a din arose. The bewildered beast walked towards a saloon car, whose owner, startled by warning shouts, moved it quickly; then the rhino turned and passed close to the chairman's car, went slowly towards the river and finally disappeared into a thicket. I was relieved to see its good behaviour, as rhinos particularly when provoked are most unpredictable beasts.

Billy took this occasion to give the chairman a letter asking him to allow the operation on Jespah to be performed. Immediately after the release we left the Serengeti.

When we reached the Mangara Escarpment on our way to Arusha, the sun was setting; in the fading light the expanse around us seemed boundless. Suddenly we heard a sound of humming and the notes of an instrument, which sounded like a xylophone, and there, walking across the immense plain, was a small toto, playing a home-made instrument, consisting of a few bars of thin metal of differing lengths fixed across a hollow wooden box. As the little boy walked out into the darkness, it seemed to me that Africa was his, or he was Africa —maybe he was.

Next morning Billy attended the Arusha Conference and afterwards the Chairman of the Trustees, Sir Julian Huxley, Peter Scott, Noel Simon and some other guests lunched with us and we did our best to persuade the chairman to agree to the operation on Jespah being performed if this became possible and necessary. We did not succeed.

After this failure, we had a private conference and Noel Simon felt so strongly about the matter that he wrote to the chairman, expressing on behalf of the East African Wild Life Society his concern at the situation which had arisen in regard to Jespah. He was particularly anxious that the present explosive situation should not deteriorate and perhaps result in a grave setback to the cause of wild conservation in East Africa, in which Tanganyika had always played a leading part.

He therefore suggested that Dr. Harthoorn should be allowed to examine Jespah and if necessary operate; that for this purpose George should be allowed to accompany Dr. Harthoorn on a ten-day search for the cubs and that during this period they should be given facilities for finding them and permission to feed the cubs if this seemed necessary. Finally he said that I had agreed that if these concessions were given, I would not ask for any more privileges and would therefore leave the cubs to fend for themselves. I added a note to the letter confirming what Noel Simon had said and agreeing that if the chairman wished it, I would not accompany George and Dr. Harthoorn on their expedition to find the cubs and operate on Jespah: thus giving proof that my insistence that Jespah should be found did not arise from a selfish motive.

Next morning to end our sightseeing we went to Ngurdoto crater, a small extinct volcano, which had recently been added to the national park. From its rim we watched hundreds of buffalo and more wart-hog than I had ever seen before wandering about its swampy bottom. Then after a series of disastrous breakdowns we eventually managed to motor back to Nairobi and Billy caught his plane for Europe.

When I got back to Isiolo I found George there. The rescue team had been successful in removing forty-four kob to the Mara Game Reserve. They had decided to wait before attempting to remove the rest of the herd who had got to know the range of the cap-chur-gun (from which the immobilising drug was shot at them) and had become very shy.

George had news that Elsa's grave had been wrecked by elephant and rhino, so we set off to investigate, taking with us the slab of stone on which her name had been cut and a bag of cement to make the cairn elephant-proof.

When we got there we found the damage much less than we had expected. But rhino had obviously used it as a resting place, two of the euphorbias and all the aloes had been eaten, and the bush along the river bank and in the studio had been trampled flat. I found elephant and rhino droppings everywhere.

I had dreaded going back, but now felt strangely at peace, almost as though I had come home. I walked along the river hoping to meet some of our old friends, such as the baboons and the bushbucks but the place seemed devoid of game. Only when the sun went down did I hear the morning warbler give his call and after we had gone to bed, the genet cat arrived. She came into George's tent, helped herself to some cheese and behaved as though we had never been away. George took some flashlight photographs; she seemed quite at home and only left with her piece of cheese when he came very close.

Next morning we drove to the Big Rock and collected lorryloads of large slabs, which we broke off the surface of the rock and rolled down the steep slopes. We wanted to build up the cairn, cover the stones with slabs and cement the whole invisibly together. At the head of the grave we intended to place the black slab on which Elsa's name and the dates were engraved. As we needed to send the lorry back to Isiolo to fetch more cement, we took the opportunity to get more aloes to replace those which had been eaten.

The country was very dry—was this the explanation of the absence of practically all animal life or had poachers driven them away? We only saw a couple of baboons which were extremely nervous; probably it was hunger that had caused them to appear within our view. One of these used the pegs driven into a baobab tree by some honey hunter, as though they were the rungs of a ladder. He was after the large fruit of the baobab, which is filled with pulp and often used by Africans to make a cooling drink. I was glad to see that the parrots were still nesting in their baobab tree. There was no sign of the Fierce Lioness and such lion droppings as we found near the Whuffing Rock were very old. This confirmed the report of the game scout who had seen her pride up river two months ago.

For a week we worked at Elsa's grave and during this time the unusual stillness seemed unbearable. Only at night we occasionally heard elephant calling up river and the genet cat came to visit us. When we had finished building up the cairn, we piled a strong thorn enclosure round it and left for Isiolo.

Here we heard that the meeting of the Trustees of the Serengeti had been put off till the end of October. This was worrying as the rains begin in November and though the park is not then closed conditions would be very bad for a search. All we could do was to wait till we heard the trustees' decision. Noel Simon was the first to hear it and he rang up to tell us that our proposal had been turned down. He was as much distressed as we were.

If in August we had realised what was going to happen we should have made the most of the good weather and continued our search. Now it was 30th October and we should have to race against the rains to get to the Serengeti and try to find the cubs before conditions made movement impossible. No one could prevent us from going on with our search provided we complied with the park regulations applicable to tourists.

In the N.F.D. the rains had already started and we had a lot of difficulty in getting our two Rovers and the Elsa lorry along the flooded road which led to Tanganyika.

Meanwhile Billy Collins had sent the director a cable expressing his concern at the situation and asking whether George and a Serengeti park warden might not be allowed to camp out in order to discover what condition Jespah was in. The reply received from the chairman gave the reasons on which the trustees' decision had been taken; they were briefly as follows:

1. Jespah, when last seen by us on 12th July, was stated to be in excellent condition.
2. The veterinary adviser to the board believed that the arrowhead would work its way out and quoted the case of a horse owned by one of the trustees that had had a similar accident

and carried an arrowhead embedded in its rump for over two years without affecting its condition and that the arrow had fallen out without any interference.

3. The operation might cause injury to Jespah and would be a setback to the cubs' taking up a truly wild life.

4. The cubs might have wandered away and our searching for them would disturb the wild life in the park.

We felt that the trustees should not base their assessment of Jespah's condition on the over-optimistic telegram which George in his relief at finding the cubs had so lightheartedly sent off in July, as we had made it clear to the director when we stopped at Arusha that once we had had a chance of observing Jespah it became obvious that he was in fact very unwell.

Nor did we think it realistic to compare a domestic herbivore with an arrow in its rump with carnivore who, in order to eat, must hunt with unimpaired physical strength. Naturally we had no wish to have an operation performed on Jespah unless Dr. Harthoorn considered it essential in order to avoid a worse handicap, and so far as disturbing the game was concerned, we believed that our remaining stationary by night would cause less disturbance than the movement of tourist cars by day.

The thought of Jespah's condition was a constant worry to us and as for Noel Simon, he took the matter so much to heart that when the Director of the Serengeti National Park asked the Wild Life Society to support the decision of the trustees, he told his executive committee that if they did so he would feel obliged to resign.

While all this was happening we were in the Serengeti under an overcast sky which threatened to release floods at any moment.

We camped at our former site. The plains were teeming with large herds of wildebeeste and zebra and there were many foals and calves amongst them. When we went to the cub valley we were held up at its entrance by the lioness who was blind in one eye and whom we had seen before. She lay in the track and wouldn't move, so we were obliged to drive round her. In the ravine we found no trace of lion but when

we drove on to the parkland valley, we saw a pride of five at a
zebra kill and among them two young lions, one with a short
blond mane and another with one equally short but darker.
We remained there for four hours watching the pair until we
were quite sure that they were not Jespah and Gopa.

We thought that one way of attracting our cubs might be by
leaving our empty car out overnight by the ravine. The
familiar sight might attract them and if it did so, next morning we would recognise their spoor; or they might even wait
for us. We therefore placed my car where it could be seen
from a long way off and then went home in George's.

That night it poured which delayed our start next morning
and later we were held up by finding four lionesses with six
very small cubs at a kill near the head of the cub valley. We
stopped to watch them and soon noticed that we ourselves were
being watched by a fifth lioness who was hiding behind our
car. We had never seen so many female lions together but
assumed that the male must be close by.

On our arrival at the ravine we found no lion spoor near
the car and decided to leave the Land-Rover where it was for
some time so we protected the wheels with thorns and removed
the spare tyre, because hyenas are not averse to eating rubber.

When we got back to Seronera we found that we had missed
the director who had been there during the afternoon. This
was disappointing as four days earlier, on the 9th November,
there had been a meeting at which our problems had been discussed.

On our daily searches we saw many animals with their
young. Several of the local lionesses had newly born cubs
which looked most endearing as they shook their wet fur between the cloudbursts; we saw also a couple of small cheetah
cubs with their mother near the ant-hill where Billy Collins
and I had seen the particularly handsome cheetah. Everywhere
topi and kongoni fawns skipped about, making one jump after
another on their stiff legs and looking as though they were
propelled by springs. Though kongoni can outrun many
animals it was difficult to understand how such young animals

could have the strength to keep up this means of locomotion over long distances.

By now the rains had set in properly and flooded the country. In spite of the difficult conditions, we crept up valleys, and into the hinterland beyond the escarpment, but we never saw a sign of the cubs. We covered about one hundred miles a day. Every morning we went to the ravine but usually saw only the lioness with the blind eye.

On the 9th of November the director and his wife came to Seronera and invited us to dinner. He was anxious to buy Momella, a farm adjacent to the Ngurdoto crater which would make a valuable addition to the national park and we all drank a toast to the success of the scheme. After dinner he took George aside and told him that it was the precedent of the horse with the arrow in its rump that had been one of the main factors in deciding the trustees to refuse permission for Jespah to be operated on and added that in spite of there being differences of opinion at the meeting he hoped it would all end amicably.

By now it rained every day and nearly all day, and we were often bogged or had other misfortunes; once we burst two tyres while trying to cross a bad lugga and as we were changing them four buffalo watched us from much too close for my liking. On another occasion while we were working in pouring rain to fill in a muddy rut with brushwood and jack our car out foot by foot, two lions circled around us giving low whuffs.

Next day we got completely stuck. George harnessed himself to the block and tackle like a mule. One end of the thick rope was tied to a tree, the other cut deep into his shoulder. Nevertheless he got us out of the sucking mud. I steered and two lions whuffed very close to us. The morasses churned up at the drinking places by elephant and buffalo showed us that we were not the only ones to suffer from the boggy state of the ground and that animals too were finding movement very difficult.

It was no longer possible to drive and even the high ground along the base of the escarpment was in a bad state. Sometimes we got stones to put into ruts; at others we were able to find a termite hill and place its hard cement-like substance under the wheels; but in the end we were always obliged to resort to the block and tackle procedure.

We had a small compensation for our disappointment in not finding any trace of the cubs by being able to observe the reactions of various animals to the rains. One afternoon we saw a pack of hyenas hanging round some burrows which we had known for a long time but had never seen occupied. They must have had underground ramifications for now we observed animals disappear down one hole and then reappear from a burrow some hundred yards away. Among the hyena pack were a number of cubs who behaved like little jack-in-the-boxes, poking out their heads and then, when they saw us, popping back immediately.

A few miles farther along were twenty-two wild dogs, whose young seemed quite unafraid of us. Much darker than the adults, they romped about giving short, hoarse barks. Close to Seronera we came upon a pride of thirteen lions with nine cubs one of which was obviously ill. It didn't go with the others for their evening drink or suckle its mother, who went over to it, smelled it, pulled a grimace and walked away; leaving it sitting a hundred yards from the others looking miserable and being sick. Later a couple of the cubs stalked it and prodding it invited it to play—the cub didn't respond but the three were still lying together when we went home.

Certainly lions have much more affectionate family life than other animals. Hyenas, for instance, which always seem to be on the prowl, show little love for each other.

That evening we invited to dinner two American photographers who were camping close to us. They had been travelling through the African game reserves for twenty months. The rain pattered on the canvas, but we were dry and cosy inside the tent. It rained all night; nevertheless we went off next morning in search of the cubs. To avoid getting bogged, we kept, as much as we could, to the tops of the ridges and found that the few animals which were about were doing as we were.

However, a moment came when we were obliged to cross a lugga. Almost at once, the car got completely stuck in muddy water right at the bottom. The banks were so steep and so slippery that the tyres could get no grip on them, so it wasn't the engine that was going to get us out.

As there was no tree to which George could attach a rope and lever the car out, he sank a heavy log a foot deep in the ground and rammed two cross bars against it hoping it would stand the strain, but it didn't. Now he stuck several thick logs in at short distances from each other and wound the rope round them. This device might have worked if a fresh cloud-burst had not come and softened the ground still more.

After this our last hope seemed to be to pave the banks with pieces of bark and branches and trust that this would enable us to drive the car up them. We worked frantically, for we did not want to get benighted in such a spot, but each time we thought that we had made a surface on which the tyres could get a grip and drove forward the Land-Rover slid back. The water was rising and had reached up to our waists. It was very cold and we were frozen. Just before it got quite dark, George decided to have a last try at heaving us out. But as he pulled with all his strength on the rope, it broke and he somer-saulted backwards into the icy water.

All we could do now was to spend the night where we were.

George settled himself in the back of the car and I made myself as comfortable as I could on the front seat, from which I kept an anxious eye on the water which was still rising and was by now about at the level of the seats. Luckily we had a Primus stove with us. George lit it and dried his soaking clothes on a line over it. We spent a most disagreeable night and the irony of it was that, after pleading for so long to spend a night in the open, so as to attract the cubs by keeping our headlights on, now that an accident had obliged us to pass a night in the open, our position, at the bottom of the lugga, was such that our lights could not be seen at any distance.

As we sat, tired, stiff and cold, it was tantalising to hear two lions calling and to know that even if they were our cubs, they would get no message from our lights to let them know we were there. Besides these two lions we heard an elephant trumpeting close by.

When dawn broke, George made some tea, which warmed us up a little and gave us the energy to renew our efforts to get the car out of the lugga.

George tried every trick he knew to heave the car out, while I walked a long distance collecting bark and branches to stick into the bank.

About 11 o'clock our hopes rose for we heard the vibrations of a car engine and hoped this meant that someone was looking for us, but very soon the noise faded away. Soaked to the skin, we went on working in the pouring rain till 3 p.m. when we decided that as after 28 hours we hadn't managed to move the car one inch we had better start walking back to Seronera. We were exhausted and it would be a long and dangerous walk, but better than spending another night in such awful conditions. We were just starting off when a Land-Rover arrived and out got one of the Americans who had dined with us two days before. He told us that when we didn't return our boys gave the alarm and two cars set out in search of us, but the heavy rain had obliterated our spoor. It was one of these cars which we had heard during the morning. Now even with a lot of pushing and towing it took us two hours to get clear. Then all three cars splashed home to Seronera. That evening we celebrated our return with a bottle of horrid sherry; it was the only drink we could buy, because owing to lack of transport all stocks were in very short supply. The shop usually got its stock by lorry from Arusha or Lake Victoria, but since the roads had become impassable everyone in Seronera had been obliged to tighten their belt. Indeed at one moment the food position became so serious that the park warden decided to risk sending a Land-Rover to Ngorongoro for supplies. We suggested that Elsa's four-wheel-drive lorry should accompany this car, since it could carry petrol drums and bulky food packages; and besides with two vehicles to help each other, the risk of getting stuck would be less.

No one could remember such awful rains and it was estimated that 75 per cent of the animals had moved to the higher slopes of the Ngorongoro crater to escape from the swampy plains. We knew that lions were taking part in the exodus and wondered whether our cubs were among them.

The unprecedented floods often imprisoned us for days on end and camp life became very uncomfortable; the canvas got saturated and in my small tent everything was damp. We placed buckets by the tent poles to collect the rain as it ran off, in the hope of preventing the ground from turning into a bog. The buckets had to be emptied repeatedly and during the night they overflowed so that each morning I was obliged to wade through puddles which had formed on the ground-sheet.

In the evening thousands of insects swarmed around the lamp. In particular flying termites shed their nuptial wings all over the place and the smaller insects succeeded in finding their way inside our mosquito nets, even though we had tucked them in and used Aerosol. Once this invasion began we were obliged to turn off the light and I lay freezing in my bed as icy gusts of rain hit the tent and drizzled through the leaking canvas—what would I not have given for a hot-water bottle.

Even birds found the weather trying. One morning I watched a pair of red-rumped swallows trying to build a nest inside my tent. They flew to a tent pole with lumps of mud in their beaks and tried to stick it on to the wood but the surface was too smooth and the mud fell off. I tied a piece of string round the pole to give them a better grip; delighted with this they went on building and had nearly completed a cup-shaped nest when a heavy storm shook the tent and the nest broke up; discouraged, the red-rumps abandoned the remains of their home.

During the days in which we were marooned the only game we could watch was a pride of lions with many young which lived on the nearby kopje. Amongst them was a cub about five months old; it had a growth like a thick roll which stretched from its neck to its forehead. The deformity didn't seem to hamper the cub who was a lively and affectionate little animal. Several times he came up to our car, tilted his head as Jespah does and then disappeared into a cleft in the rock, but soon came back accompanied by three very small cubs, whose coats had so many dark markings that they looked almost black. The older cubs bounced on them, rolled them over and licked them and it was plain that they were great favourites with the other youngsters. Later the older cubs went off and climbed up a tree but as there wasn't enough room for so many of them each got pulled off in turn by the tail to make room for the next. Tails always played an important part in all their games and attempts to catch and bite another cub's tail often ended in a spanking match, but it was all very good-natured fun.

When the cubs came very close to us, their mother, plainly considering this reckless behaviour, placed herself between us and them; instantly the cubs rolled with swishing tails and waving paws all over her. We watched them for many days, then one afternoon the cub with the growth was missing and we never saw him again. We were very concerned about him as we thought that a playful bite into his growth might have caused a fatal hæmorrhage since such growths are full of blood vessels.

By now the lorry and the car were overdue and a tractor was sent out to search for them; they were found bogged down but all the supplies were rescued.

When conditions allowed us to make another attempt to reach the ravine to see how my car was faring we found the plain deserted, except for a pair of ostriches with seventeen chicks who paraded across the marshy ground on their stiff legs, looking as though the place belonged to them; and indeed, there were only a few jackals to keep them company, four of whose cubs we found diving in and out of the holes of an abandoned ant-hill which they were using as a burrow. Like lion cubs these youngsters seemed to be naturally clean and always left their playground to defecate. They were grey or side-striped jackals, a species we had never seen before. They came close to our car and were very inquisitive. Farther on we saw a pair of adult jackals on a Tommy kill; they left it when we approached and it was instantly covered by vultures. Then, like lightning, the jackals rushed back with flattened ears and scattered the birds. One dragged the meat off and began to tear at it as fast as he could before his mate returned.

We did not reach the ravine that time for we got bogged down and spent the rest of the day digging ourselves out.

When we returned to the lodge we learned that Prince Philip was due to visit the Serengeti on the 11th and 12th December and that during his time there no one except the staff would be permitted to remain in the park.

The weather continued to be appalling; there was very little game about and the lions near the lodge, which had been joined by another pride, had to go considerable distances to find prey; as a result, the cubs who were too young to accompany their mothers were often deserted for as long as forty-eight hours. When the lionesses as well as the cubs became emaciated the park warden sometimes shot a buck to prevent the mother from having to abandon her children while hunting. This helped the Seronera prides but I wondered how many new-born cubs far away from the lodge would survive these conditions.

As I was suffering from toothache and anxious to see a dentist in Nairobi I was glad that a plane could land in such weather and that I was able to get a seat in it. The parts of Tanganyika and Kenya which we overflew were one vast swamp; floods had carried away bridges and buildings, roads were impassable and near the coast the Tana and Athi Rivers had swept over whole villages and turned large areas into lakes: the conditions made it obvious that it would be extremely difficult for help to reach the victims of the disaster. The floods were still rising and I wondered how Kenya and Tanganyika would ever recover from this catastrophe.

I spent five days in Nairobi and then flew back bringing a winch with me; next day when we went to the cub ravine it proved its worth, for we were able to extricate the car from any hole in a short time and could therefore drive along places which we had till then thought too dangerous to risk.

On our way we met six little bat-eared foxes with their mother; it must have been an unusually large litter for all were the same age. They sat in a line, pricking their absurdly large ears, staring at us and looking like toys. Suddenly the whole lot of them dived into the nearest holes and we saw a hawk soaring in the sky. Only when he had flown away did the little foxes dare to peep out of the burrows. Having assured themselves that all was safe they then scampered into the open and played like kittens about ten yards away from their mother. We thought it was probably because their burrows were cold and wet that they came out in full sunlight which is not their usual custom.

It was a month since we had left my car in the ravine but as the rains had washed away all spoor we could not tell whether the cubs had been to inspect it. Hoping for better luck we left it where it was.

We drove ten miles down the valley but saw no game except buffalo. Tsetse were present in swarms and the canvas of the car was black with them. We disproved the theory that they only follow moving objects, for even when we stood still we were covered with them and however long we waited they showed no sign of taking-off.

On the 6th December two park wardens called to tell us that in connection with Prince Philip's visit we must leave Seronera from the 8th to the 13th and suggested that we should spend this time at Banagi, eleven miles away and on the border of the park. We asked whether we might not be given special permission to continue to look for the cubs during the days that the Duke was not spending in the park, but the director did not grant it. So we moved to Banagi.

Until Seronera was built this had been the headquarters of the Serengeti. Its one house, formerly the home of the game warden in charge of the Serengeti, was now used as temporary accommodation for people doing research work in the park. In memory of Michael Grzimek a laboratory has been built near to the house which it is hoped will one day become a centre of scientific research. Both buildings stand on a small hill overlooking the river which one has to cross to reach them. A cement causeway makes the crossing easy in dry weather but when there are floods communication with Seronera is only preserved by a bamboo bridge which hangs from trees that grow on opposite banks. It had not been used for some time;

the ladders up to it had disappeared and the bridge itself hung at an angle of forty-five degrees towards the river and there were many gaps in it.

The house had a large, open veranda in which a colony of little swifts had built their nests in clusters of ten to forty. These were made of grass and of the downy feathers of rollers, guinea-fowl, weavers and other birds. Towards evening the birds flew in large numbers swiftly round the house, justifying their name. As soon as we lit the lamps a few of them usually banged their heads against the windows till they landed on the floor. Picking them up to restore them to their nests, I felt their fragile bodies tremble and to calm them stroked them gently. To my amazement they not only settled down, but bending their heads and closing their eyes went into a kind of trance and I had to pull them off by force, so tightly did they grip my hand with their spiky curved toes.

During the first night it rained without stopping and we could hear the rising river roar. It seemed that we had got to Banagi only just in time to cross the causeway.

Next morning we explored the neighbourhood and found the muddy ground around the house full of lion spoor. About half a mile away was another large river which by now was a raging torrent. Quite as impassable as the one nearer the house and since it had to be crossed to reach the border of the park, we realised that we were now completely cut off.

All we could do was to write our mail and listen to the wireless on which we heard an appeal from the small Somali village near Elsa's camp for help in fighting the floods. Only a hundred yards from the house a buffalo had taken up his quarters and until we were told that he was an old-established resident we were surprised that although lions roared round nearby he never moved off.

On the 13th of December we watched the cars of the Prince's party, accompanied by the chairman, the director and three park wardens, passing along the far side of the river. The Duke left the Serengeti that day. Anxious to collect our letters and send off our mail we sent a runner to Seronera. He crossed the bamboo bridge, walked eleven muddy miles and

waded through a flooded river to accomplish his task. Amongst
the letters he carried was an order for a squeeze-cage. Having
read *The Circus Doctor* by Dr. J. Y. Henderson, the chief
veterinary surgeon of Ringling Brothers and Barnum and
Bailey Circus (U.S.A.), we realised that to operate on lions with
the minimum of danger this type of cage was an essential. It is
made of strong wire mesh and when a handle is turned one
side is slowly moved by rollers towards the imprisoned lion,
and the animal is thus rendered immobile without being hurt.
After corresponding with Dr. Henderson we had decided to
order a squeeze-cage in Nairobi, so as to have everything ready
for the day when we hoped to get permission to operate on
Jespah.

By the 15th a labour gang had repaired the damaged causeway and we returned to Seronera.

After our return we went to the cub ravine where we saw the
lioness with the injured eye; she watched us calmly for a
quarter of an hour. She didn't look like Little Elsa but to
make sure we called all the familiar names and waved her
pie-dish at her. But she only continued to look at us and finally
she disappeared into the ravine. It was strange that a wild
lioness should have remained so long watching us, but
probably she had cubs in the ravine which she was guarding.

As I was suffering from malaria I went to bed when we got
back to camp and through the roaring chorus of lions who
seemed to be very close I listened to a splendid broadcast of
the *Rosenkavalier*, an unusual accompaniment, the only
occasion on which I have heard my two favourite concerts
simultaneously.

Next morning we saw a small herd of zebra and noticed that
one of them had a humped spine and a body about eighteen
inches shorter than that of a normal zebra. It was a mature
animal and seemed in perfect health. We had often seen
animals with goitres and other minor deformities, but never
anything to compare with this freak and thought it interesting
that the deformity seemed to have had no harmful effect on
the zebra's health.

Now I must confess that during my last visit to Nairobi I

had been so depressed about Jepsah that for the first time in my life I had consulted a fortune-teller, a man of great repute. He told me that on the 21st December my stars would change and with them my luck and that I should be unexpectedly successful. (I assumed in finding the cubs.) He added that during the critical period I was to wear something blue, for this was my lucky colour. I was rather ashamed of myself and didn't tell George what I had done but I did keep a blue handkerchief on me by day and by night, and on the 21st I felt excited. That morning we decided to try to reach the ravine but came upon a vast lake which had formed over a salt-lick. George tested it by wading in up to his thighs, then he took off the fan belt and drove the car into it. Almost at once, we stuck and the water rushed up to the level of the seats. As fast as I could I took off my clothes, grabbed the cameras and waded out. In my hurry I forgot my blue talisman and when I looked back I saw my handkerchief floating away and with it my belief in fortune-tellers. We spent all the rest of that day working to get the car out, so it was not till next morning that we were able to go to the ravine. We found my car still there; we checked it, and then drove fifteen miles down the valley, but saw only a giraffe and a couple of hyenas. The tsetse were in full force and the going was so rough that the back axle of the car broke. When in the evening, rattling and slushing through the mud we reached Seronera, we were greeted with cries of 'Here comes the submarine,' a name which stuck to George's car. I went to bed early but woke at about 5 a.m. and heard two lions whuffing near the kitchen. I turned quickly so that I could watch the opening of my tent. A few moments later a heavy body brushed against the canvas and pulled out several tent ropes, then a large lion came in and stood within a few feet of my bed; with his great mane he looked like a giant powder-puff. Luckily there was a camp table between us which gave me time to yell. At my shouts the lion jumped back, went out and rejoined his friend. Both trotted past George's tent, but kept on whuffing for a long time; they were probably intrigued by the light of our torches which we focused in their direction. On the following night the pair came again to visit us but I heard them in time to shout and prevent them from calling on me. They walked between our tents and then disappeared into the night.

George's car had to go to the workshop for much-needed repairs, so on Christmas Eve we got our lorry to take us to the cub ravine where my car was still stationed. When we reached it the driver went home in the truck and we drove on in my car.

It rained without stopping and we saw no sign of the cubs, so, towards evening, turned home very dispirited. When we came to the river we found that it had risen rapidly and was now 8 feet deep. This meant that we were cut off from Seronera and should have to spend the night out. It would be very uncomfortable but perhaps it might give us the chance we had waited for for so long, of attracting the cubs with our headlights. We parked in the open as far as we could from the river and left the lights switched on.

They attracted millions of mosquitoes and other insects, and, as we had no Aerosol, we were completely at their mercy. All I could do was to put a cloth we had used for cleaning the windows of the car, over my face to protect it.

Twice we heard lions roar and hoped the cubs might come. But only a hyena appeared. She showed great interest in our rubber tyres and was not at all alarmed by our shouts, but bolted when she got our scent. I lay on the front seat remembering how we had spent the last two Christmases. Christmas Day 1959, when Elsa had suddenly reappeared for the first time after giving birth to her cubs and had swept our Christmas dinner off the table in her joy at seeing us again; and Christmas Eve 1960, when she and the cubs had watched me light the candles with so much interest and Jespah had gone off with my present for George and I had opened the envelope which contained the deportation order.

To-day bore no resemblance to those days and in the morning when I wished George a Happy Christmas, he looked surprised and asked: ' Is to-day Christmas Day?' All the same, I was glad I had spent last night in the car rather than in camp; but George felt that we should try to get back to

Seronera at once, so as to prevent a rescue party from setting out to look for us and wasting petrol of which there was very little left.

The river had fallen during the night and with some trouble we managed to cross it; soon afterwards we plunged into a deep hole and I hit my head so hard that I saw stars, but not the favourable stars which the fortune-teller had promised me. Afterwards I felt sick and I had so bad a headache that I thought I must have concussion.

When we arrived in camp the boys told us that all through the night lions had been around, and the ample spoor we saw corroborated this story.

A big Christmas mail was waiting for us; presents had come from all over the world : several of the donors had taken the conditions in which we were living into account, so besides having many nice things to take back to Isiolo, our camping from now on would be much more comfortable. Later in the day, we went for a walk, listened to the brightly coloured buffalo weavers singing in chorus and we were fascinated to observe a scarabæus beetle, less politely known as a dung beetle, walking backwards, moving a ball of dung with its hindlegs and pushing so hard that its head was bent downwards nearly to the ground. These iridescent bluish-green insects deposit their eggs in fresh dung; this they roll into a ball and later it serves as nourishment for the grubs. Our beetle had a mass almost as large as a golf ball, which it was rolling at such a pace that it often lost its balance and tumbled over.

Farther along we saw a strange formation of pale-coloured termites. They looked like sticks, measured about a centimetre and were arrayed in several parallel rows around their hole. We thought this must be a defence formation and events soon proved that it was so, for a stream of fierce safari ants appeared. Instantly the termites stiffened and the majority of the safari ants, although they were twice the size of the termites, at once turned back. The termites spat at the few stragglers who remained behind, ejected a sticky substance which probably affected the respiratory organs of their vic-

tims for after a few wriggles they died. We examined one of
the termites and found that between its mandibles it had a sort
of syringe through which it ejected the liquid.

It was a lovely evening and we saw a strange phenomenon
which we had sometimes observed in the semi-desert areas of
the N.F.D. As the rays of the setting sun faded out in the
west, in the east there appeared a reflection of the sunset,
rather blurred but otherwise an exact replica.

We continued hunting for the cubs from dawn to dusk,
and observed that the wild animals were gradually returning
to the valley. Among them were three lionesses with five cubs.
Thereafter we met them so often that they became quite
accustomed to us and one afternoon when the lionesses went
off to stalk a buffalo they left the cubs to 'stay put' so close
to the car that we could easily have picked them up.

Though no lions again visited me in my tent at Seronera
there were many about and one evening the boys pointed out a
pair sitting in a bush about seventy yards away. They growled
for a while and later one came and sniffed at my tent, but
trotted off when I shouted at him. We shone a torch at him
and saw his eyes reflecting its light. Fond as I am of lions,
when this sort of thing happens I am very glad if George is
nearby. During these nights he was often visited by a genet
cat who came in after the large fat whisky moths. These
moths have got their name for the fact that they usually
appear at sundown and drink from every moist bottle neck or
glass. We had little enough alcohol to give them but in spite
of this they appeared in swarms as soon as it got dark and
when George turned his light out the genet cat came to hunt
them. It was a welcome guest but we felt much less hospitable
towards a hyena who at first stole only jam, butter and biscuits,
but eventually got away with eight pounds of cheese and all
our sausages and bacon, which had only just arrived and were
our great luxuries.

George did his best to shoo the hyena away but it continued
to be a perfect pest until a pride of lion came on the scene and
took over the camp. There were six or eight of them. Two

lionesses were particularly persistent visitors. George focused his torch on them and told them to be off, but they only blinked at the light, and remained standing twenty feet from us. When they moved it was only to join their half-grown cubs who were noisily lapping the bath water which we had put in a bucket to use for cleaning the car. After quenching their thirst they settled round George's car, which was parked next to his tent and through the night he could hear them moving within a few yards of him.

For a short time the weather improved, then the rain returned with renewed force. Our only chance of finding the cubs was to look for them on the higher levels. So, as far as the floods permitted, we decided to make a thorough search of the hilly area. To reach it we would drive across the plains, keeping where possible to the ridges.

We recognised that our chances of finding the cubs were not great, since in that vast area covered with rocks and woods, and broken up by cliffs and rivulets, one might easily pass within a few feet of a lion or any large animal without seeing him. Already we had several times nearly collided with a group of buffalo wallowing in a mud pool, concealed by the shoulder-high grass. On these occasions I held my breath wondering what the outcome would be, but the huge beasts proved as anxious as we were to avoid an encounter; they emerged as quickly as they could from the morass and cantered away tossing their great heads, only giving a few backward glances to see whether we were following them.

The ground was terribly soggy and as disagreeable to the animals as to ourselves; we had proof of this one morning when we saw a lioness and her two cubs high up in a tree obviously trying to keep dry. As we came up to take a photograph, the little ones fell to the ground, then the lioness jumped down but immediately led them up another tree. On this trip we also saw a very amusing sight: three jackals being chased by angry guinea-fowl. Whenever the jackals turned the cackling birds flew over the trio or pecked at them. At this the jackals rushed off with their tails between their legs to a safe vantage point from which a little later they made a counter-attack, but the fowl grew so aggressive that finally the jackals bolted.

During all these weeks the rains never ceased and our 'submarine' gradually fell to pieces; the centre bolt went, the U-bolts, the brake pipe, the starter, finally the exhaust pipe broke off, yet, in spite of this, the car continued to carry us until the day when we were again marooned in our camp by the floods. Then I used the car as a bedroom, for my tent was leaking like a sieve and anyway perhaps it was prudent to sleep there, as a pride of lions with five cubs had settled very close to the camp. One morning we found them on a topi kill not more than a hundred and fifty yards away; that evening we were expecting the lodge manager and his wife for drinks; I walked along the track to meet them and when they arrived got into their car. As we drove back we saw the pride standing on the very spot at which I had waited a few minutes ago for our guests.

Chapter Nineteen

THE WIRETAILS

DURING OUR 'imprisonment' we had the swallows for company. A pair of red-rumps were making a second attempt to build a nest inside my tent; and, as I wrote, flew over my head plastering mud on to the pole. Then one morning a rival pair appeared. These were wiretailed swallows and most attractive with their thin elongated tail feathers and red head-markings; they were smaller than the red-rumps. Having first surveyed my car as a possible site they eventually decided to build inside my tent. For a day the rivals flew in and out, twittering excitedly; then the red-rumps went off and the wiretails took over. I provided them with string to help them get a better grip on the pole and they built busily, quite unperturbed by the noise of my typewriter, though they flew off if I moved quickly, or if George or one of the boys came in. They worked from first light until it got hot, returned at tea-time and went on building till it was dark. I observed that they reinforced the structure with bits of grass which they dipped in mud before attaching them to the nest. The female was much more industrious than the male who often had a rest on the ropes and preened himself. It took eleven days to complete a well-shaped open cup close to the tent canvas.

Next morning the pair used the tent rope for a mating display which they repeated several times during the day. In the intervals the hen bird collected small feathers and grass with which to line the nest. I helped her by putting out some tufts of cotton-wool; these she picked up three at a time and I had to replace them quickly to satisfy her demands. Four days later I held a mirror above the nest and saw three whitish eggs covered with reddish-brown spots. It was only after the clutch was complete that the hen started to sit on them. Then, for seventeen days, she sat devotedly, only leaving the nest for short periods during the hot hours to feed herself. As far as I could observe the male never came near her during this time. The young swallows hatched out just a month after their parents had started building the nest. (Eleven days to build, three days to lay, and seventeen to incubate.) On that day I found an egg on my camp-bed which stood under the nest; thinking it had fallen out by accident I waited till the birds went out to feed, then, with the help of a mirror, I replaced the egg in the nest, which I now saw contained two baby birds. They were still wet and quite naked and with their enormous yellow-lined bills they looked very ugly and very pathetic.

Soon after the parents came back I found the egg again on my bed; evidently they knew that it was not going to hatch and wanted to get rid of it. They took it in turns to keep the youngsters warm and only left them towards midday when it was very hot. On the second day the chicks began to develop a fine fluff. From now on their parents were kept busy from morning till night catching enough insects to satisfy their ravenous appetites and even when I approached the nest the big bills opened hopefully. The little swallows kept their nest spotlessly clean; how they did this I do not know, for during the first days I never saw them perch on the rim to drop their excrements, though the bed below was covered with droppings.

Soon after the birth of the chicks the tent was badly shaken by gusts of wind; the nest started to sag from the pole and then a very heavy rain storm flooded the camp. Next morning I was woken by the mother swallow twittering in great agitation and fluttering up and down between the canvas which was slightly lifted and the mesh wire of my car sleeper. I rushed into the tent and found one of the little birds, lying on the bed, gasping and very cold. I picked it up and breathed on it, trying to warm it. I then saw that the front of the nest had broken off and that the remains were dangling on a few strands of grass which were likely to break at any moment. The other fledgling was still in the damaged nest but there was now no space for a second bird, nor enough rim left for the parents to perch on when feeding their young. I was very much impressed by the reasoning power of the mother bird, who, when she found that the disaster was beyond her capacity to tackle, had come at once for my help. Calling George to hold the little bird in his hand and keep it warm I quickly collected some Cellophane tape and stuck the nest together, then I made a sling out of a pillowcase and attached it to the canvas on either side of the tent, thus giving it a support. While I repaired the nursery the parent birds flew round my head, watching all I was doing. My fear that they might be frightened by the white sling proved unfounded, for as soon as I had finished they took over.

The only change which the accident gave rise to was that from that time onwards the parents deserted the nest during the night; however, as by then the fledglings were beginning to develop feathers, they were able to keep each other warm. One grew much faster than the other. We thought he was a male. When he was sixteen days old he started to parachute from the nest but could not take off from the ground to return to it. His urge to fly was greater than his ability and his parents seeing his plight used to flutter around nervously until I picked him up and replaced him in his nest. Then the performance would start all over again. Unfortunately, even after dark he was restless and one morning I woke to see the parent birds sitting quiet and motionless on the tent rope, and going into the tent found the little bird dead on the bed.

To guard the remaining chick, which I took to be a female, I remained in camp and let George go off alone to search for the cubs. This was just as well for she chose that day to start trying her wings. Like her brother, she could parachute down but was unable to rise again and I was kept busy putting her back into the nest. When it got dark and the parents went off, I placed her in a small box lined with soft cloth and kept her near me. Next morning before dawn I put her back in the nest and when the parents arrived at first light they found her waiting as usual with her bill wide open asking for food. That day I again remained behind to watch over the little swallow. The parent birds never left the fledgling but could do little for her but chase off the butcher shrikes which pin baby birds on

to long spikes and then eat them. The fledgling could by now
fly about a hundred yards but was still helpless when she had
reached the ground. There were a lot of sparrows round the
camp and she was frightened of them, so I tried to keep them
off by feeding them at a distance with the maize and grass
seeds that had collected on the car's radiator. They were of
course delighted and were soon joined by a family of mice
who fed so near the birds that they often actually touched each
other.

Compared with this gay little party the swallows had an
anxious time protecting their young whose vulnerability
astonished me; when George told me that he had found a pair
of wiretails nesting in a mudbank overhanging the river, I
could not think how the parent birds were able to prevent the
fledglings from drowning if, on their first flight, they landed
in the river.

Next day, when our parent birds arrived at the nest in the
morning they flew close but no longer fed the little bird and
were evidently inviting her to follow them. After a little
while the fledgling plucked up courage and flew in a straight
line to the top of an acacia tree. Then, although her wings
and tail feathers were still very short and she found it difficult
to keep her balance, she flew from tree-top to tree-top, the
parents following closely and feeding her. At sunset the
parents got very excited and tried to make the youngster return
to the nest; they even shook the twig on which she was perch-
ing. But, the harder they tried to make her move, the more
determinedly the little swallow clung to her twig and when
it became dark the parent birds left her. I too did not know
what to do, for I had no means of reaching the top of the tree
to catch her.

During the evening George and I went several times to see
how the fledgling was getting on and always found her
bravely holding on to the same twig. The nights were cold and
we feared that she might die of exposure or fall a prey to
nocturnal enemies, but when dawn came and I went out to
see how she was, I found her still on the same twig and
apparently none the worse for her night out. Soon afterwards

the parent birds arrived; all that day they kept near the fledgling and fed her as she flew from one tree-top to another, but they seemed nervous and came several times into my tent as though they wanted to attract my attention and perhaps they wanted me to catch the youngster and put it back into its nest.

For five nights she struggled on, flying each day a greater distance from one tree-top to another, followed by her parents. We tried to imagine what caused her to choose to remain alone at night in the cold and danger. Of course, she did not know where her parents spent the night and perhaps she did not realise seeing the tent from outside that her nest was inside it, nor that my car contained the box in which I had placed her at night. Was it possible that some atavistic instinct made her reject the man-made contrivances in which she had been reared and impelled her to stick to the trees, where by nature her nest might have been?

On the morning of the sixth day I saw her puffed up into a little ball, with her head tucked into her shoulders; she was quivering and when the parents appeared with food she didn't open her bill or her eyes. Thinking that she was only suffering from the cold of the night I believed that the warmth of the sun would put her right and did not attempt to reach her. But very soon the parent birds flew into my tent and around my head in great distress, so I went out and saw that the fledgling was still in the same position. George got a ladder, I went up it and with some difficulty managed to catch her. She had no external wounds but was shivering and did not open her eyes. I carried her to the nest hoping that the parents would feed her but they remained on the tent ropes and did not come near her. Suspecting that they were frightened of me, I left them alone for a short time; when I came back I found the little bird struggling on my bed, I replaced her in the nest and then saw a small clot of blood inside it and wondered whether she might be suffering from pneumonia. A few moments later she again fell on to the bed. After this I kept her in my hand and tried to warm her by breathing on her. But finally the little head sank and she was dead. I laid her on the bed. Then, a most extraordinary thing happened; the red-rumped swallows which had never put in an appearance since the wiretails had starting nesting, suddenly turned up and chased the wiretails from all round the camp. This went on for several hours and the red-rumps seemed to be the victors as they perched on the tent ropes and the wiretails flew round the trees.

But the next morning the situation was reversed, for the red-rumps had gone off and the wiretails were busily collecting mud for a new nest. As we were going to be obliged to leave the Serengeti during the rainy season which would coincide with the incubation period, I could not bear to see them wasting time and mud on building a nest inside a tent which would soon be removed, so I took away the string and the other building facilities I had provided for the first nest. I felt very unhappy as I did this and still more unhappy next morning when the pair perched on the ropes and sat watching me looking bewildered. Finally they flew off and never returned. For many weeks when I had woken up the first sound I had heard had been their twittering. Now I found the silence so painful that we began to set off on searches at the first streak of light before the time at which the swallows used to come. I have told this story consecutively although it upsets the chronological sequence of my diary, because this is the only occasion on which swallows have nested in one of our tents and I have been able to observe the rearing and fate of a family. It is a sad story, for the parent birds had been devotion itself and the fledglings were so happy till the male chick died nineteen days after it hatched and its sister six days later. The little bird's resistance to five icy nights had made her seem almost symbolic of life to me. In watching her I had found comfort in thinking that Elsa's cubs like this little bird were in the call of God. How was I now to interpret this tragedy? I was moved by the way in which the parent birds in spite of all the devotion they had expanded on the chicks now accepted their death and with extraordinary resilience started immediately to prepare for a new family.

Living close to wild animals for so many years I have come to find that their instinctive reaction to fate is often very

superior to our own and that theirs is a wisdom I still have to
learn. In this context I had been recently much impressed by
the way in which a spider I watched coped with her difficulties.
I cannot feel any affection for these eight-legged creatures but
I was fascinated to observe this spider remaking her com-
plicated web each time the rain destroyed it or it was torn by a
large insect; whatever the source of the disaster she went to
work at once to repair the damage and she had courage as
well as patience: she would often tackle beetles many times
larger than herself, wrapping them in her silky thread until
they were tied up like parcels and ready for consumption.
Watching her, I hoped that we might be capable of learning
from this low form of life how to show an equal determination and persistence in coping with the problem of the cubs
and, in particular, in fighting my distress at not being able to
find them and help Jespah.

Chapter Twenty

THE PRICE OF FREEDOM

WE HAD now struggled for months against the worst possible weather, wrecking our car, putting important work aside and doing no good to our health and all this under conditions which greatly reduced our chances of finding the cubs. So, when on the 2nd of February the director came to Seronera, I wrote to him repeating my plea to be allowed to sleep out since this was our best hope of seeing the cubs. He replied that it was not within his competence to give us such permission but that he would place my request before the trustees at their March meeting if I wished him to do so. By then Jespah, if he were still alive, would have carried the arrowhead for a year, unless it had sloughed out. Since, for the time being, we could do nothing more to obtain the permission we needed we continued our search, trying desperately to find a route by which we could reach the escarpment and its hinterland. We drove from dawn to dusk, over most difficult terrain, forcing the car up steep rocky slopes, jerking from boulder to boulder, and often banging our heads against the roof when we fell into deep holes. But only when the rains had decreased did we eventually succeed in reaching the top of the escarpment and even in driving along it. The early morning and late after-noon were the most probable times for seeing the cubs but it was difficult for us to reach the area where they might be early enough, or to leave late enough because of the need to obey the park regulation, that is, to be at Seronera during the hours of darkness. This meant a fifty-mile drive across extremely rough ground.

Once we found a small lion cub by itself in the open plain; it was so young that it might easily become the prey of any predator, even a jackal; we discussed whether to take it to the park warden so that he could release it to a pride with cubs of the same age which might adopt it, or whether to leave it where it was in the hope that in time its mother would return to it. We waited until dark; then we informed the park warden and early next morning we all went out to look for the cub but found no trace of it and we could only hope that the lioness had come back and that it was safe.

When conditions became more normal some lions gradually followed the game back to the valley. Before the rains we had thought nothing of meeting twenty-five or thirty lions in a day; now if we saw nine we were greatly elated and our hopes of finding the cubs rose. We felt sure that we should recognise them not only because Jespah's and Gopa's manes would still be much shorter than those of other lions of the same age, but also because of their individual characteristics, which even if they had split up and joined another pride, would make them identifiable.

About this time Peter Scott and his wife called on us. He was particularly concerned that the tension between us and the trustees should not be publicised in any way that might diminish the financial support received for the conservation of animals. I fully agreed with him and pointed out that with this in mind I had refused to be interviewed by the Press and had stopped a public petition, promoted in the United States, to support our request to be allowed to sleep out and to let a veterinary surgeon, helped by George, operate on Jespah should he be found in a condition which warranted such an intervention. We parted agreeing that whatever our personal views might be our first consideration was the survival of wild animals.

One evening the director again visited us and I suggested that as a possible way of breaking the deadlock I would be ready to attend the March meeting of the trustees if it were thought that by doing so I could clarify the position. The director promised to let me know if this could be arranged. The camp manager, who had come with him, told us that two days earlier when he had approached the shed in which he kept his Land-Rover a lioness jumped out of the open back of his car and that to-day she had repeated her performance. Evidently she was seeking shelter from the rain; but in future the camp manager proposed to keep the canvas drawn over the back of his car.

After some days I learned that the trustees had agreed that I should appear at the meeting, so, when the time came, I started off for Arusha, leaving George to search for the cubs. As I drove across the plain I saw that great herds of wildebeeste and zebra were returning to it from the high ground. While it had been devoid of game we had not searched the area, but I thought that when I returned we must see whether our cubs might not be among these herds.

The executive committee of the Board of Trustees consisted of the chairman, three trustees and the director; a veterinary surgeon was there as a guest. I asked to be permitted to sleep out and if we did find the cubs to be allowed to decide afterwards what it would be best to do about Jespah. My request was turned down on the advice of the veterinary surgeon who had never seen Jespah, and on the evidence of the telegram George had sent in July, saying that we had found the cubs in excellent condition. I pointed out that as soon as we had time to observe the cubs more closely we had retracted this statement so far as Jespah was concerned, and I stressed that many people who were qualified to judge the case of a lion carrying an arrowhead had supported our view that an intervention might be essential. I added that these were people who would not risk their reputation unless they were sure of their facts. It was of no avail so we found ourselves back where we had been for the last nine months. Before I left, my attention was drawn to the fact that the Serengeti would be closed during the next rainy period—April and May—but that should we wish to come back in June as ordinary visitors, there would be no objection.

When I told George the outcome of the meeting he decided to appeal to the Minister of Lands, Forests and Wild Life of Tanganyika, and wrote to Minister Tewa asking for permission to sleep out and also to continue our search in the Serengeti during the rainy period.

The reply was negative. The Minister referred to the trustees' decision, to the tragic death of the young farmer which had occurred last year and to the lesson to be learned from it. He added that he and the trustees had an overriding duty to allow nothing which might imperil the safety of the visitors to the Serengeti and that there could be no shading of this responsibility, and concluded by saying that the trustees had advised him that their decision was necessary in relation to the promotion of safety, so he felt bound to accept it.

Our conviction was that whereas a healthy lion practically never attacks human beings a lion handicapped in hunting could be a danger—and also that since we had obtained a squeeze-cage and an offer of help from one of the best veterinary surgeons in East Africa, the intervention itself would not involve any risk. But we were in no position to argue.

During the time that was left we determined to concentrate our searches in the areas which were free of tsetse and should it prove necessary, we would return in June and continue to look for Jespah. When the park warden returned from a safari he told us that he had seen the lame young lion which a white hunter had also recently seen. He was still in company with another lion who was plainly providing him with food, since he could not hunt for himself. The park warden had shot two Tommies to help him out, but doubted if he would recover and said he meant to keep an eye on him and put him out of his misery if it seemed necessary. On hearing this, even though the warden had assured us that the lion could not be Jespah as he had no wound or scar, we set off at once to find the injured animal. On our way we met a safari party who told us that they had seen two very thin young lions one of which limped. We did not think this could be the warden's pair for they were ten miles away from where he had observed them and the lame animal could hardly have covered such a distance. As we drove on we looked out for this pair but saw no trace of them. When we reached Naabi Hill we came upon a party of three balloonists. They had started from Zanzibar and ended up in the Serengeti where they were experimenting with the possibilities of game observation from a balloon. Now they were packing up and all we saw was the small wicker gondola in which they had floated. I couldn't help picturing what might have happened if they had been up in the balloon near a water hole and a lion had taken a fancy to the ropes, as well he might, and smartly detaching them from their moorings had started off across country with the helpless passengers in tow.

We asked them if they had seen any lion and they told us how one had climbed a tree quite near to their tent and how another had gone off with one of their blankets. This had resulted in a tug-of-war; they were keeping the blanket to show off its holes.

Within a few hundred yards of Naabi Hill were some rocks and a few trees which provided shade and made the spot an ideal lie-up for lions; from here they could watch the surrounding plain which was now teeming with game.

We found the rocks occupied by two young lions. George had seen them before; then one of them had been ill, but now both were in fine condition. They rubbed their heads affectionately against each other just as our cubs always did. Nearby was a fully grown lioness; when we stopped the car to take a photograph of her she rolled on her back with her four paws in the air and yawned lazily.

We drove on through thousands of Tommies, zebra, Grant's gazelle, and wildebeeste amongst which we saw a flock of over a hundred ostrich chicks led by a single cock. This was quite a wingful to be guarded only by one cock, and he seemed aware of his responsibility, for he charged away at top speed, giving us little time to take a picture. Although ostriches are well known for their large number of chicks we had never before seen such an enormous nursery.

Though the plain looked quite flat it was in reality broken up by many shallow waterpans; in the banks of these the hyenas had made burrows in which they lay in cool comfort well concealed from the game that came to drink nearby. At our approach, they hobbled out of their shelters and we counted as many as ten emerging within a few yards of each other.

One morning we saw a young blond lion and three lionesses on a kopje; they let us come close to them, and the lion, though he seemed older than Jespah, looked tantalisingly like him and I could only hope that one day he too would have his harem and be equally happy. When we saw the pride again late in the afternoon they were in the plain and evidently selecting a prey for their evening meal from among a group of three zebra and a foal which were grazing unsuspectingly about four hundred yards away.

One of the lionesses advanced, her belly close to the ground; after thirty yards she stopped to let the rest of the pride catch up with her; the lion brought up the rear. Then a different lioness took the lead and led the party forward another thirty yards. They were within seventy yards of their prey before one of the zebra noticed them. The lions, seeing they had been spotted, froze; the zebra looked calmly at them and continued feeding. Meanwhile the foal moved towards the pride as it grazed. Everything around was quiet and peaceful and it was distressing to see the little zebra so innocently approaching the lions; they seemed to be in no hurry and just sat in a line, watching. Well, the lions had to live and who was to criticise them for killing in order to survive; indeed, I could remember a time when I thought it great sport to shoot a defenceless deer. That was long ago and after I had lived for some time close to animals in their natural environment I could no longer imagine how I had once been capable of taking the lives of harmless creatures simply to provide a trophy for my vanity.

When the light faded we had to drive home so we were spared seeing the end of the stalk, but perhaps the foal escaped, for next day when we came to the place expecting to find the pride on a kill, there was no carcase nor were any lions to be seen. A few miles farther away, we found three lionesses devouring a freshly killed wildebeeste. One of them was carefully removing the hairs of the beard and spitting them out. She reminded me of Elsa, who always detested tickling hairs and feathers and although she loved guinea-fowl refused to eat one unless we had first plucked it for her.

In the afternoon, we had a chance of seeing the ceremony observed by wild dogs on rejoining their pack.

We came upon eight at their burrow and noticed a ninth rushing towards them. He arrived panting, greeting each member of the pack in turn by rubbing himself against it; when he had finished his round he moved away and defecated; then he came back to rest with the other dogs. Later four more arrivals took place, each dog behaved in exactly the same manner. We were therefore convinced that this greeting to all members of the pack by a returning dog and the marking of the burrow with excrement, must be customary with wild dogs—it was a habit we had never before had the chance of observing.

Circling round Naabi Hill on our way back, we saw a pride of eight lion and stopped the car; immediately a young male rushed up and sat close looking at us. He was so strikingly like Jespah that we even wondered whether he might be our cub, but he showed no scar and his expression was different. All the same we wanted to test him, but could not wait to do so because of the need to be back at Seronera by nightfall.

Very early next morning we set out to look for him again. The pride had only moved a short distance into the plain; they were dozing and too replete to bother about us, except for the young lion who came up, circled the car and behaved in such a friendly manner that doubts again assailed us. Could he be Jespah? The pie-dish would be the conclusive test. We held it out: the cub looked at it with complete indifference. Then his brothers and sisters plucked up courage and came to play around the car and we had to resign ourselves to the fact that these were not Elsa's children, though the largest male cub had many characteristics in common with him, including the habit of keeping watch over the pride whilst the adults rested and recovered their energy for the night's hunting. Once this young lion had satisfied himself that we were harmless he went over to his father and snuggled up to him but, head on paws, continued to watch us through half closed eyes, long after the rest of the pride had gone to sleep.

By now we had almost given up hope of finding the injured lion, though we were anxious to do so, to make quite certain that he was not Jespah; one day, we found him by a rainpool. His companion was with him, and not far away were two young lions with short ruffs. The four seemed to have formed a bachelor party; we hoped it was for the purpose of helping the sick lion. At our approach he pulled himself up into a standing position, but carefully sat down again for obviously it hurt him to put weight on the injured leg. His rump was withered, he was very thin, and the expression of his eyes showed that he was in pain. A first glance had told us that he was not Jespah, but I was tormented by the idea that our cub might be in a similar state. We would have liked to have shot a buck for the invalid and had asked if we might do so should we find him in distress, but were told that we could not have permission to make a kill. We therefore left him hoping that his companions would provide for him.

We had not much time left before we should be forced to leave the Serengeti for two months, so as we knew that by now we had investigated the lion population round Naabi Hill pretty thoroughly, we decided to spend our last days examining the cub valley. The animals had by now returned to their normal habits and the area was well stocked with game. We were therefore astonished to find three lionesses with four small cubs at the end of the valley, for this was a pride which we knew well and had previously seen forty miles away. Although in three or four weeks they could easily walk this distance, knowing how lazy lions are, we were puzzled to know why, when food and water were in plentiful supply, they should have undertaken a long trek. Moreover, they had been well established in their territory, so it seemed unlikely that they had been chased out of it by another pride. All I could imagine was that they had moved away from the tsetse which had come to their area during the rains.

Their movements were of particular interest to us since we hoped they might give us some clue to the movement of our cubs. George believed that they had been chased away by other lions, while I believed that the floods and the tsetse were more likely to be the cause of their disappearance. The behaviour of this pride seemed to confirm my views. Of the many beasts we had become familiar with in the cub valley, the impala ram in the ravine was our oldest friend.

When we reached the lower end of the valley we saw that the tall borassus palm-trees by the river were heavy with bright orange fruit, the size of ostrich eggs, and that a flock of emerald-green love-birds were nesting in them. Fascinated, we watched them flying between the fanning palm fronds while on the rocks close by a troop of baboon disported themselves. The elder males squatted at some distance from the females who were suckling their young, grooming their fur and occasionally spanking a boisterous infant.

On our way home, we noticed some circling vultures and, driving in their direction, came upon a couple of lion on a buffalo kill. They were mature lions and if it had not been for this difference in age we should have been convinced that they were Jespah and Gopa, for the blond lion had the same narrow, long muzzle, golden eyes and an equally good-natured and dignified expression as Jespah, while the darker of the two had a squint like Gopa. But they were at least four years old, with fully developed manes, so it was impossible that they should be our cubs.

On the last lap of our way home, we stopped to investigate a strange monkey which peeped at us out of some foliage. His reddish coat and long tail proved him to be a Patas (red) monkey, an attractive species rarely seen in East Africa. Then, bumping along in a hurry, for we were late, we suddenly found ourselves face to face with three sleeping rhino; luckily before they could stagger to their feet we had circled round them. I had never been so close to rhino before and hope I may never be again.

During our final days in the park we drove non-stop from sunrise to dark hoping that we might still get a sight of the cubs before we had to leave. We had spent five months in the Serengeti, much of it under appalling weather conditions, we had driven ceaselessly, making demands on our bodies and on our vehicles that they were scarcely able to endure, we had searched every accessible place in which we thought the cubs might be. It had all been fruitless. The only positive results were that we had got to know the wild animals in the area and been able to study their behaviour during the rains and we left a network of car tracks that would be useful to the wardens in reaching hitherto inaccessible parts of the Serengeti.

On our last day we were again guided by vultures to a buffalo kill near to the place where five days previously we had seen the two lions that looked so like an older Jespah and Gopa. To our surprise there they were, once more devouring a buffalo, though why they should choose to tackle these formidable beasts instead of the vulnerable kongoni and smaller antelopes we could not understand.

The dark lion who resembled Gopa, replete to bursting point, was guarding the kill against three cheeky jackals, who seized every opportunity to sneak a bite, till a growl sent them running off to avoid a cuffing. The blond lion took no part in the defence, but lay in the shade of a tree, his mane ruffled by the morning wind.

How splendid these lions were—aloof, but friendly, dignified and self-possessed. Looking at them it was easy to see why the lion has always fascinated man and become a symbol of something he admires. The king of animals, as they have called him, is a tolerant monarch; true, he is a predator, but predators are essential to keep the balance of wild life and the lion has no wish to harm, he does not attack man unless he is persecuted for his skin or when he is too infirm to find other more active prey. He never kills except to satisfy his hunger as it proved by the unconcern with which herds graze around a pride when they know that the lions' bellies are full.

How I loved watching this scene in front of me. I thought of Elsa's children. Where would they be at this moment? My heart was with them wherever they were. But it was also with these two lions here in front of us; and as I watched this beautiful pair, I realised how all the characteristics of our cubs were inherent in them. Indeed, in every lion I saw during our searches I recognised the intrinsic nature of Elsa, Jespah, Gopa and Little Elsa, the spirit of all the magnificent lions in Africa. May God protect them from any arrow and bless them all and their Kingdom.

Serengeti, June 1962